Chains of Life

Volume 1

WILLIAM JOE ADUSEI

Copyright © 2019 By William Joe Adusei
- ISBN13: 9781619570085
- ISBN10: 1619570084

BISAC: Religious/Inspirational
All rights reserved.
No part of this book may be reproduced or transmitted in any form or by any means, electronic or mechanical, including photocopying, recording, or by any information storage and retrieval system, without permission in writing from the copyright owner.
This book was printed in the United States of America.

Dedication

To the righteousseeking yet struggling servant of God out there.

Table of Contents

Acknowledgement 11
Introduction 13
Preface 15
Biography: I am WHO I am not Who He Is 17
Roasted Corn and The Move of the Holy Spirit 21
The Pungent Yet Refreshing Scent 23
Ut Unum Sint (Latin: That They May Be One):
The Myth and the Reality 25
The Hotness of The Pepper Is in
The Eating and The Pain, In Its Shitting 29
Jesus And the Alliance for Coup d'état 31
My Admired Lady on The Stations of The Cross 33
The Humanity of the Inhuman 35
Gazing at the Mountains from the
Valleys of St. Hubert Seminary 37
Amitabh Bacchchan but Not Indian 39
The Bitter Yet Sweet Tastes of
My Lady CoTenant's Tongue 41
Mr. Ecclesiastes, Ghana Says You Are Wrong 43

The Gem in the Sand: Thankfulness in the
Face of Challenges... 45

A Dog Called "Obofuor" (Angel)........................ 47

Fr. Dorr's 'Son'.. 49

The Holy Ghost Congregation:
My Pharaoh or My Paul?...................................... 51

OWASS (Akatakyie Boys) and The Holy Communion 53

Scenes of Austria And the Grace of God............. 55

The Vandal Crown but Not Vandalistic Character 59

Room B10, Commonwealth Hall and the Case of Paul 61

In the Football boots of Barcelona FC................. 63

Stupid Diplomats Under Abuja Street Lights 65

The Drumbeats of KKD....................................... 67

The Little Elephants in the Jungle of St. Louis............ 69

The Captured Promise by the
Pine Trees of Aburi Botanical Gardens................. 71

The Mission Boy's Fears...................................... 75

The Tears of My Broken Palm Wine Calabash............ 77

The Cassock of Piesie and the Boxing Gloves
of Mohammed Ali.. 79

First Class Flight from Gilgal to Jordan................. 81

My Daughter Lydia, King Herod and
Anas Aremeyaw Anas... 83

The Voice of John the Baptist or the Uplifting of Satan? 87

The Sacred Mantle of Hotep Ra:
Blessings for Us but Not Others?......................... 89

The Gods Turning Around in a Musical Chair?............ 91

Why Should I Vote for a President?..................... 93

Sailing in The KBL Ship and Swallowing
the Unswallowable 95

The Mystery of Okomfo Anokye and
The Reality of Jesus Christ.. 97

Trip to My Spiritual Family 99

The Succulent Breasts of Mary, the Mother of Christ. 101

River Twobiri at KunsuWioso and
The Greatness in Life 103

The Vandals Are Coming 105

A Vandal! And So, What?. 109

The Nuclear War Between the Mind and Eyes:
A Torture for the Head. 111

In qua regione facta sunt nostri, aut non audisti? 113

The Tragic Voices of Tragic Heroes. 115

On the Bus: Temptation from The Devil or
Self Inflicted Adventure? 117

On Stage with Kofi Denis, Jutta, Job and
Alan Paton this December 119

The apostles of Accra Haasto and the Church in Berea 121

Moses and Family Planning Methods in Midian 123

The Two Fire Fighters on The Battle Lines of
The Samaritans. 125

The Virgin Mother Mary Weeps from Abu Dhabi. 127

Sin to Save 129

Alexander Fu Sheng & The Snake Fist. 131

The Dead Fowl Fight 133

Not for Me. But for Them 135

When Kumasi Took Over Takoradi 137

The Appian Way At SAHUUS. 139
Qui Se Ressemble S'Assemble: Birds of
The Same Feathers Flock Together. 141
David! David! David! 143
Where Is Bepo Yaw, The Smoking Mountain? 145
Upon the Wings of Lucky Dube 147
Our City. Who Is to Prophesy?. 149
Abraham's Quota: Is the Situation All That Bad?
What about the 7000 Diplomats?. 151
Oh Lazarus! Oh Ohenenana Angela. 153
The Possibility of the Impossibility. 155
The Dark Colored Blood or the Yellowish Cooking Oil? . . 157
Not Extra Time Yet 159
The Father's Mantle 161
Neutralizing Moses' Weapon of Mass Destruction. 163
Takoradi Show Boys and The Chariots of Pharaoh. 165
Sitting Under the Ladder with Jacob 167
The Cry of the Toddler or the Emptiness of the Vitro? . . . 169
Eliphaz Said It All 171
Tempus Fugit (Latin: Time Flies) 173
The Wings of Togbe Beyond the
Walls of the Vandal City. 175
The Milkmaid Girl and The Diploma's Daughter. 177
The Sailing Ships of Don Diego d'Azambujas and Co. 179
Embarrassment in The Lord? 181
Good Friends We Had, Good Friends We Have Lost 183
Tunes in the Grave: Kelvin Kuofi 185

Chorus of the Aged 187
President Nana Addo and Herod's Gift of
John the Baptist's Head 189
Protocol Officers. 191
From The Tomb of Arimethea
to The Mountain of Galilee 197

Acknowledgement

It is tricky to mention names when you are coming to or in public. Out of bitterness, anger, disappointment and frustration you could be tempted to mention names. But when it comes to something good, there is every possibility that you would offend someone, i.e. when you fail to mention people you should have mentioned. This is so because every individual whom we cross paths with, at any point in time, contributes, in most cases, to our wellbeing knowingly or unknowingly. For this reason, I have decided to restrain myself here. But to do justice to humanity, myself and people out there, I would venture to mention three names. With some sense of comic relief, I have decided to choose all three from the feminine species. Names that represent

- People (males, females, relatives, friends, school mates, coworkers, loved ones, church members, household neighbors, etc.),
- Feelings (affection, gratitude, pain, disappointment, guilt, inadequacy, etc.)
- Situations (lack, want, desire, betrayal, victimization, encouragement, etc.).

As to who they are, who represent what, and what each individually means to me, I leave that for another time. For now, take them to represent you out there who are reading me. So, without any special order, and also not in line with the generic groupings I have stated above, here I go with (no titles);

- *Lydia Adusei.*
- *Susan Efua Sackey.*
- *Juliana Afuwmwaa Nanka Bruce.*

Introduction

For a very long time, God's race has always been merciful to me by maintaining His gift of life for me even in situations when I should have been dead by now. I have come to realize that, among other things, this grace is to enable me to fulfill His own divine mission commissioned for me even before my birth. The mission, as revealed to me several times and in different forms, is to open the doors of people's destiny unto fulfillment. Like Jonah, I have had cause to stay away from this mission *(Jonah 1: 13 RSV)*. Yet, He has always sounded to me His clarion call to 'put on these priestly garments and go out there to do my work'. Who am I? Moses complained and sought to stay away from his call not knowing God had made him a 'god' unto his own brother Aaron and Pharaoh (Exodus 4: 14-17). So, though I am a mortal here on earth, I also now see myself as a great key in the hands of the Unseen One to turn around the doorknobs of people's lives. In what form? Well, herein lies one of them; this book and its contents.

Preface

Fr. Anthony Kwadwo Osei, Seth Tenkorang (a.k.a. Ecoute), Maame Anima, Sappiro, Lena Okon, Siduu, Billy Theophilus, Eric Akosah and Okyere Bona are just few of the many voices who called on me to make this work public. This is a compilation of daily selected posts that I shared with readership on my WatsApp platforms between April 2015 and June 2018 (daily posts of three years). Unfortunately, when I finally decided to heed the call and make this compilation available, I could not retrieve most of them. When I was posting on the WatsApp platforms, I did so with the idea of sharing them there and then. But then most of my readership, some of whom I have already mentioned above, felt the pieces worth compiling in a book form. But due to technical mishap I could not lay hands on those I had shared in the early stages. I however appreciate my old time Six Form 'A' Level school mate, Okyere Bona, who came out on his own and told me he would want to publish them for me. I haven't set eyes on him since we left school in 1984. Just few months ago, out of the clouds, he connected with me through the advancement of technology whereby he made his publication proposal. I appreciate this offer. What constitute this compilation therefore are only those selected from posts between July 2017 and June 2018 (just one year out of three years daily pieces).

These compilations, captioned Chains of Life relate to issues that cut across all fields of life though most of them are written against the background of biblical principles and under the mirror of biblical events and texts. I could have quoted right away the scriptures to drum home my messages. But instead, I sought to do so by narrating them within contemporary life experiences. These experiences are mostly those of mine. In presenting them, I do not intend to attract attention to myself. Neither do/did I intend to discredit any person who finds himself/herself in the narrated accounts. Names of persons and places mentioned are therefore real and not fictional or twisted. They are written without any biased inclination to any particular sex, religious faith, ethnicity/nationality, etc. though they are mostly set within the Ghanaian context. They are 99.8 % my personal life experiences.

Because I am dealing with all ranges of readership, I did not restrict myself to any particular academic style of writing especially in relation to grammar. In some, they are 'raw' grammatical expressions (English) and, in some, attempted phraseology. In some instances, I have had to chip in Latin and French phrases, which I would say, perhaps, it is my nostalgia to my youthful days at the seminary to become a Catholic priest, a quest I aborted along the way. In the seminary, the study of Latin was compulsory, and I really enjoyed studying it.

The views I have put across here are my personal views. You are obliged to agree or disagree or throw them disdainfully into the dust bin. But it is my hope that greater part it, if not all, would be welcomed wholeheartedly. Amen.

Okyere Bona and Team, I am grateful for all your sacrifices and hard work in seeing this work through.

Biography:
I am WHO I am not Who He Is

They kept coming to me, from individuals and from groupsplatforms at different types. I responded to them but now and then, they would resurface. They are questions that mostly bothered on my Christian status and dispensation. So, I deem it fit to once again sum them up and make them available here. At least, it would help you appreciate the background against which I have written these pieces. So here we go.

- *What is the name of your church/Have you established a church/where is your church?*

    No, I haven't established a church. Like the Apostle Paul, I associate myself with Fellowships that God leads me to depending on the location I find myself in. Over the years, I have held the belief that I should work in the secular field and support the ministry work instead of me enriching myself from God's work. But I am now thinking of establishing my own fellowship which would focus on teachings.

- *Are you a Catholic priest?*
    No. Though I was once a (Catholic) seminarian of the Holy Ghost Congregation/Fathers, I dropped out on my own out of certain personal convictions.

- *Do you sometimes regret not becoming a Catholic priest?*
    Not at all! Fortunately for me, I still have good relationship with my ordained colleagues. In terms of doctrines, I still hold my Catholic faith though some find this confusing because I associate with and minister at nonCatholic churches. I find it a great privilege to be a good and responsible father. The Bible says we are created in the image of God. So, if I produce children, then I am producing God

- *Where is your church in case somebody wants visit?*
    I haven't set up a church of my own.

- *Are you an ordained Pastor of any other affiliated church if not a Catholic priest?*
    I strongly believe in the evangelical institutions. As Paul once asserted, Peter was sent to the Jews and he (Paul) sent to the Gentiles. So, I minister and offer my teachings with churches where I find myself. And to give full recognition to this role after many years of operation, I was ordained as a Pastor by a network of ministries under the Healing Outreach Chapel International in Takoradi. Let me quickly add that I am currently based in Kumasi and now lead the Friday morning teachings and prayer sessions at the Our Lady of Apostles Catholic Church at Gyinyase, Kumasi.

- *Do you work on your own or affiliated to another church that pays you?*
    I am not and never on any church's payroll. I minister on voluntary basis.

- *What is your profession if not a fulltime pastor?*
My (secular) profession, which spans over a period of more than 25 years, has been in various disciplines in technical cooperation (NGO) sector. But I have been out of job for about two years now. So, I am now restrategizing my career; full time teaching ministry work or combine with the secular.

- *Are you based abroad or in Ghana?*
In Ghana, though with occasional travels abroad in the past. After about 22 years sojourn at Takoradi (Western Region of Ghana), I have now relocated to Kumasi here in Ghana few months ago.

- *How does one contact you?*
Email: joeadus@yahoo.com
Mobile: +233 (0) 244611900
WatsApp: +233 (0) 206384695

- *Would you accept invitation to minister when invited?*
Yes.

I hope the above few tips answer all question pertaining to my Christian values. More would be provided in the messages compiled in this book. Enjoy the full blessings that God has designed for us, even as He has led us to His throne of mercy through Christ our Redeemer.

Roasted Corn and The Move of the Holy Spirit.

Pentecostal convocations, crusades, anointing sessions, impartation programs, etc. In just a few days to come, the Christian world would be commemorating the outpouring of the Holy Spirit on the early Christians, Pentecost Day as recorded in the book of Acts 2. This set into motion the zealous venture by the early church to carry out the Great Commission of God to bring His message of the good news of God's salvation through Christ. And it is this zeal that also eventually brought the 'adventurous' missionaries to this part of our world, though some have questioned the morality of these missionaries. But what is of good case of reflection is the demonstration of their willingness to brace the storms to see to the establishment of churches among us. They battled with diseases, hunger, thirst, martyrdom, and all sorts of grave inconveniences. I learnt many years ago that some even lived only on roasted corn, what the Akans call "nkyewe3"(NOT popcorn) and water only on their trips to the interior. They did not concern themselves with anointing to perform miracles, ostentious lifestyles, apostolic titles, number of people they attract to their anointing sessions, show offs, psychedelic postures, manipulations, etc. (Even those missionaries who came in later years like the SMA, the SVD, the

Holy Ghost Frs. of the Catholic church) Yet, it is these moves of theirs over the centuries and decades that have now given us the arena to boast ourselves as (modern day) bornagains, Dr. Dr. Soandsos, Bishops, "Apostles", Prophets, "angels", private jet owners, miracle workers, breakthrough crusades/gatherings, etc. God and his mission have now been pushed far away from us. Where is the core value of salvation in the church now? Let's be careful we do not get whipped/punished, instead of being empowered, by the Holy Spirit even as we get "crazy" organising all sorts of activities in his Name.

The Pungent Yet Refreshing Scent

There are these food substances of the Asantes of Ghana which are of particular interest to me: *momone and totobi*. "Momone" is sort of fresh fish but treated with salt and served as a seasoning ingredient for sauce/soup. "Totobi" too is the cow hide which is processed by intentionally putting it in water for some days to the stage of 'rottenness' to give it a special delicacy taste. One particular feature is they give a very bad odor. In fact, a rotten pungent smell, which even from a far distance, can put you away from them. And when on sale at the market, you see flies hovering around them. Seemingly, they are unhygienic, rotten, foul scent and nothinggood about them to the outsider. But to the Asante man, a special delicacy especially with palm nut soup. Crazy smell but tasty and nutritious inside. When God asked Jeremiah to buy and put a sackcloth in a rock and later take it out, it got spoiled, useless, and appeared goodfor nothing to the physical eye, even to Jeremiah the prophet of God himself. But to God, it was a tool to serve His purpose (Jeremiah 13:1 11). Remember, Lazarus too was "rotten" in the cave. But before God, his rotten corpse was still a tool to establish the deity and uniqueness of God through Christ. (John 11:3845). If only we'd see our problems in the spiritual perspective of Christ, He'd always turn them round to the shocking eyes of humanity. Note well. The waist cloth was once beautiful and used by Jeremiah. But with time it got spoilt and "good for nothing". The same way our bank accounts have become useless because no money in them now. Our once admirable marriage has turned sour. Our once admirable properties, cars, moral life, etc. have all crumpled. For some of us our anointing and priestly unction have deteriorated. As one of my friends, Pololo, once said "Joe, even the Catholic priesthood koraa, you left. Stop disturbing us with your roadside preaching." No problem. All seems useless now, but God is ready to make all useful again. *Momone and Totobi* are rotten and of foul smell to the outsider, but they give good taste and are nutritious to those they matter to them.

Ut Unum Sint (Latin: That They May Be One): The Myth and the Reality

When the late Pope John Paul II visited Ghana in 1980, I was then at the (St. Hubert Minor) Seminary with likes of (now) Archbishop Gabriel Anokye, Bishop YeboahNyarko, Bishop Atuahene, Bishop Gyamfi, Monsignor Tawiah, Frs. Anthony Kwadwo Osei, Alexander Ansu Ebo, Kwasi Appiah, Boakye Agyemang, Owusu Addo, Oppong Mensah, etc. As part of his schedule, he was to meet and address us on campus. We were then few in population. The meeting was at the court between the school chapel and the dining hall. I was in the third year. Our seniors made sure we assembled decently. I forced myself to be at the front of my row. I knew he would shake hands with some of us and I wasn't going to miss out. No matter what our seniors would do, I would have my way. So instead of listening to his address, I was closely monitoring his lips. Cardinal Casaroli and Archbishop Marcinkus were with him as part of his entourage. They were holding boxes of rosary that he was going to give out. As soon as he finished his address and collected some of the boxes from Cardinal Casaroli, I dashed forward, grabbed his hand and took some of the boxes from him. That is how I, a young seminarian then, became a friend of Cardinal Casaroli. Back in Rome, he would occasionally send to me post cards and souvenirs. I was then staying with the late Fr. Dorr CSSp at Offinso during holidays.

Apart from the boxes of rosary I grabbed from the Pope's hands, there was also this small sort of face towel which he was holding and which I also took 'by force'. I don't know if people took particular attention to it. The words *Ut Unum Sint* were woven into it. Though I lost that token sometime later, the encounter has made me cherish those words since then despite dropping out of the Catholic priesthood voluntarily. Jesus prayed this prayer in John 17:21 for his disciples the night before His death; unity among them. But this call for unity by Jesus is also a call for all those who were/are to be His believers. In fact, it is a call for the entire world. But the question is, would there ever be world unity? I dare say, no, not until after His second coming. The unity He prayed for then, has become more of a myth but with a hope of a reality in the purpose of life. In other words, though we have differences, we could all strive together for one common purpose of welfare for humanity.

- Despite our tribal differences, we could all work together for the sake of peace.
- Despite our political differences we could put our pride aside and work for the peace of our nations.
- Instead of individual selfish desires, statesmen/politicians can limit their corrupt practices and think of the underprivileged in the society.
- Despite our different faiths, we could bury our religious doctrines and promulgate the gospel of Christ.

Yes, we may not be able to forgo our individual differences, we can still accommodate each other for the sake of humanity. Unity may be a myth, but we can make its quest lead us to achieve a common goal.

The Hotness of The Pepper Is in The Eating and The Pain, In Its Shitting

When the Ghanaian talks of hot pepper (especially those of the Akan, Ewe and Ga tribes) it means really hot. Not the inorganic ones that fall flat. But the real hot pepper, so hot that only three pieces can be seasoned with other ingredients to feed 10 or more people. I am talking about the ones which after eating and you go to ease yourself, you feel like a hot iron rod has been pushed through your anus. (Excuse my language). You take few pieces, raw ones and grind with fresh tomatoes. Voila! I like it this way. Yesterday in other not to bother myself, I settled with hot pepper sauce and boiled cassava (the soft one). I had my fourmonth old baby, Hermes, by me when I was eating. As I kept eating and playing with him at the same time, he'd kick and stick out his tongue signaling that he too wanted to enjoy some. I really wished I could give him some. But it wasn't TIME for him to enjoy this meal health wise. Maternal care advices that children should be given breast milk up to six months, though we keep on giving them foods like SMA, Lactogen, porridge, etc. But not hot pepper sauce at this time. In the same vein, no matter how old/aged we are, we are still children before God, our Provider.

So, though we may whine, cry, lament, go here and there, it is most often for our own good that we lose or don't get certain things we crave for. Yes, in the past we might have enjoyed certain breakthroughs but now find ourselves in the tight corner, God is still aware (Job 23: 811). The fact that the child enjoys Lactogen, SMA, etc. but being denied hot pepper sauce does not mean his life is lost or the father denying him. The fact that we once enjoyed good jobs, cars, foreign trips but don't get them now, does not erode God's providence. The fact that we started with Ghc2m and do not have more than that now, maybe ten years after, does not mean we are not progressing. There is a bigtime difference between 6 months when you enjoyed Lactogen and 10years when you can take hot pepper sauce. Certain breakthroughs are too hot a pepper to handle no matter our age. God might be grooming you for that. Forget about what you once, or supposed to, enjoy now. God is the Onyamkopon (the Providence Finalist), the Jehovah Jireh. That is why,

- I want WARN Men of God who raise attention to their 'power of deliverance' by plying on the distress call of people and attribute every challenge/problem to satanic attacks: witchcraft, curses, etc. You are not building to the faith in God. You are rather exalting yourselves against the throne of God. Be careful. Your end is just at the corner.

- I also want you, who believe in God, to keep on trusting God no matter how fast you might think your time is running out.

Jesus And the Alliance for Coup d'état

Something from the scriptures at church service today (Good Friday service) struck me and which has led me to propound the "Theory of the Universal Reality of Existence"(birth, growth and survival. (I hope anthropologists, sociologists and even scientists would work hard to accept it). By this theory I propound that no creature (human, animals, even trees) would want to be governed beyond measure at a point in time. It is a reality that characterizes the world we live in (I don't know of the other planets).

But of this planet called earth, that is the fact. Even God Himself would not share His supremacy with any other entity. The theory is true. That's why even in one country, more than one party compete to govern. That's why even in the same party, we may find more than 7 aspirants who would all want to be presidential candidates at the same time. That is also why even in the home, despite the betterforworse vows, the woman could at times cry out for her feminist rights and the man wanting to maintain his "I am the man of the house". To govern or not to be governed? That is the question. To me, there is nothing strange about that. BUT it is the way we allow our personal interest to pinch this fact that becomes a concern. Jesus was born into the period when his birth nation was under Roman rule. Before his rise to fame up to his death, there had been revolutionary attempts to fight against this Roman dominion, with Barabbas, who was released from treasonbars instead of Jesus, coming to mind (Luke 23:17 25). It was therefore the common interest of all wellmindful Jews, including the High Priests, rabbis, and common people, to reject the Roman rule headed by Caesar. But as I sat in church this morning listening to the long scripture of Jesus passion, from his arrest, through to His burial, something struck me. (Catholics on Good Friday read this portion of Jesus life, John 18: 140 & 19: 142, as the main gospel of three readings). What struck me? In John 19:15, when Pilate asked the Jews if they really wanted Jesus whom he referred to as "your king" to be crucified, they shouted "We have no King but Caesar", their common enemy. Because of their hatred for Jesus, they have now turned to align themselves with Caesar. Amazing. How could they sacrifice their longtime struggle for their common goal and now "eatanddine" with what they should all fight against? That is human being for you. Very tragic.

- Let me start with the church. We have Men of God/church members who just because of their developed hatred for another Man of God, go to all length to associate with people, even satanic services to work against the one they hate for reasons known to them only.
- We have political parties who go into alliances with others not because they truly believe in the policies of the newfound party. But because they hate to see their 'enemy' party come to power.
- We have people who would team up with your enemies not because they love those enemies. But just because they want to see you down.

But my caution is, before you team up with or enter into any alliance, please make sure you are doing so with a clear conscience but not to spite somebody.

My Admired Lady on The Stations of The Cross

Catholics have as one of their liturgical rites/services what we call The Stations of the Cross. These are 14 spots carved from the events related to the passion of Jesus, from the time he was condemned to death up to his burial. One of them is (the 8th Station) when Jesus met and spoke to the women of Jerusalem (Luke 23:2731). So, on Fridays during Lent season and on the very day of Good Friday, we would meditate and pray along these stations. On Good Friday itself we'd reenact these 'stations' in town to the view of the general public, not as a mere drama but a solemn way to appreciate Christ's sacrifice on the Cross. I have a confession to make here, innocent lad's confession. Some years back, there was this lady who was one of those who played the part of the women of Jerusalem. I deeply admired her. During the sessions of the 'journey', most of my attention was on her, especially the 8th Station. I didn't care much about the deep reflections we were to reflect on, the pain that Jesus was supposed to have endured. My heart rejoiced in seeing my 'admired' lady but not the suffering Jesus. Yesterday, as I joined the congregation to go through the Stations and we stood in the open sun at Gyinyase, I began to think of what was perhaps, my stupid heart's reflection in the past. I was supposedly in the presence of God, but my heart's devotion was far from Him. Deceit. Camouflage. Pretence. Cover up. But am I the only one? As a young lad, perhaps I was developing into adulthood and was bound to feel for the opposite sex. Perhaps I could be justified there. But what about those who deliberately, methodically and conscientiously plan to use the name of God for their personal needs instead of devotion to God?

- How many people have set up churches and established themselves as Men of God with a genuine cause to further God's Kingdom and NOT to enrich themselves?
- How many crusades, outreach programs, prophetic gatherings, etc. are organized without the idea to publicize our anointing and to enrich ourselves?
- How many of our priests in the Catholic priesthood who, given the opportunity, would not quit but for fear of public ridicule?
- How many people genuinely and openly make donations or support communities with genuine hearts?
- What at all prompts us to church services/programs? To genuinely workshop God? Or to primarily get ourselves spouses, visas, jobs, children, etc.? For the pardonable, we could be pardoned. But for the calculated deceit and hypocrisy, God will never forgive us!

The Humanity of the Inhuman

Psalm 116:5 and 2 Corinthians 1:35 talk of God being a compassionate One. Jesus translated this in a practical way when he healed sick people and even went on to feed 5,000 people with five loaves of bread and 2 fish. (Matthew 14:1321). I have read and heard this over and over, over the years. But I got a real sense of this yesterday. We have a male cat in our house which we have named "Fire". We got him when he was a mere kitten. We recently caused him to sleep outside the flat but in the compound. Few weeks ago, we saw the rains and floods had swept and left outside our house a poor shivering kitten. Nobody paid any particular attention. I am sure in our subconscious (mind) he was going to die so why bother pay attention to it. But few days later, we saw our grownup cat Fire going out to lie beside this kitten and play with it. We again saw Fire started bringing it to the house. Whenever they see us approach, the kitten would run away but Fire would just remain calm and come to us. Now when we feed Fire, he'd hang on till we are out of sight then he would go and bring the kitten to eat before he'd go on to eat himself. Yesterday, I was the only person around in the house. I forgot to feed Fire. He started mowing and following me here and there. When I finally gave him his food, something about him struck me. After all the mowing and scratching me, he remained calm, went and brought the kitten before both of them started eating together.

For the first time, the word "compassion" struck my heart. The humanity of the inhuman on display. If an inhuman creature like a cat can display such a high degree of compassion, what about us human beings, supposed to be of more value that other creatures? Where is our sense and practical act of compassion towards our fellow human beings? Why do we rejoice in the downfall and/or destruction of our fellow humans? Where is our sense of compassion to help our fellows who need our help? Well, if humans won't show their human nature, what about God? Surely, God would not disappoint. If He caters for the lilies of the field and birds in the air, how much more won't He have greater compassion and concern for us? (Matthew 6:2534).

Gazing at the Mountains from the Valleys of St. Hubert Seminary

Unlike so called unpleasant experiences of most people who fall out of the Catholic priesthood (seminary life), I have had the privilege of being welcomed always by my colleagues who have ended up being ordained as priests. For this I salute them all. The (Arch)bishops/Monsignors/Rev. Frs./ Gabriel Anokyes, YeboahNyarkos, Francis Tawiahs, Kwasi Appiahs, Kwadwo Oseis, Rev. Sr. Eugenia Ampofohs. I am also thrilled by the continuous show of camaderie by some, who like me, fell out along the way. The Antwi Agyeis, Fokuo Domfehs, Chaucers, Poloolos, Owusu Afrehs, Michael Appiahs, Oga Joes, Kwame Piesies, etc. This afternoon as I sit in front of my rented residence listening to oldtime highlife music (adadem) from one of the local FM radio stations, my mind captures an incident that took place one day following my dropping out of the seminary life at the St. Hubert Seminary here in Kumasi. In those days, people kept telling my parents that now that I had dropped out of the Catholic priesthood they should 'take me to somewhere' for spiritual enhancement because of the notion that if you drop out, you end up being a failure in life.

Thank God my parents never did anything of that sort; my mother in particular was worried though. May their souls find a resting place in the bosom of father Abraham. One day one of my seniors, Kwame Piesie, who was a moral support in those times, visited me and my mother expressed this concern. (I am sure Piesie himself, wherever he is now, might have forgotten this incident.) He calmed down my mother. I vividly remember his words, "Mama, Joe has left the priesthood, but I know he hasn't left God". In other words, no need to seek any other support once I hold onto my faith in God. No need to flee to any other mountains. Yes, all through my life, there have been ups and downs. But the shepherd rod of God's grace has always kept me under the umbrella of believing in Him and Him only. In Psalm 11:1, we hear of David rubbishing similar calls by his friends to 'flee to the mountains' in times of his troubles. When Satan fails to eliminate us completely, he cunningly uses those close to us, even prominent Men of God, to destabilize our faith in God. As a result, we end up throwing down our faith and resort to others. I pray that God's trusting grace continues to keep us in His tabernacle with all the stubborn faith we can and hung unto David's words when he cautions "…those who choose other gods multiply their woes." (Psalm 16:4.)

Amitabh Bacchchan but Not Indian

Some of my friends call me 'Joe Amit'. The 'Amit' refers to that great Indian film star Amitabh Bacchchan. I got that name when I was in the seminary about 39 years ago. Amitabh Bacchchan has always been my 'idol' since my youthful days (though I am yet to meet him personally). I remember a case when I dramatized one of his movies, "Kasme Vaade", which was to be staged at the seminary. I was to play the double role of "Amit" and "Shankar" (all played by Amitabh in the said movie). I managed to get one of the studentSisters (training to become nuns/Rev. Sisters) to play the role of "Suman", Amit's wifetobe. Now in the seminary in those days, as one of the strict rules, the boys were NOT permitted to talk to the girls on campus, and vice versa, though we all attended church services and classes together. (Comic irony of situation, you'd say. Very funny indeed.) So, the question was, "So Joe, how did you manage to go behind the scene and train a group of students INCLUDING a studentnun, knowing very well that the rules prohibit such an interaction?" Forbidden tree trespassed? Anyway, that is another story for another day.

Yesterday, I bumped into one of my former seminary colleagues who excitedly called me out, "Ei Snr. Joe Amit". We hadn't seen each other for ages; in fact, ever since I booted myself out of the seminary. Oh my God. I was in the company of another friend who later asked me about the Amittag. When I explained, he sarcastically remarked, "Stop being funny, my brother. Are you Indian?" Good comment. Yes, I called myself Amit as if I am Amitabh Bacchchan. But in reality, I don't have his gene, for that matter the Indian gene in me. Many of us have put Christtag on us calling ourselves Christians. But are we Christian? Take my own country Ghana for instance. Everywhere Christ, Christ, Christ. All through the week, from morning till evening, at all queer locations, even uncompleted toilet facilities, you see all sorts of christened (church) activities. But what comes out of these? Corruption, indiscipline, pride, selfishness, internal strife, etc. Like me, being "Amit" but far from being Indian, so have we tagged ourselves as Christian but living lifestyles far from His identity and qualities.

The Bitter Yet Sweet Tastes of My Lady CoTenant's Tongue.

"Is it bitter?", she asked.
"What is it?", I asked back.
"The alcohol you people take", she explained further.
"No, it is not bitter", I smiled and confirmed further.
"Then if you want something not bitter why not take in Fanta?".

That was my cotenant, a sweet charming single lady. I had that morning, some years back, told her I was quitting alcohol. So, she wanted to find out what at all was the reason behind people taking in alcohol. To her, if the reason was to taste something sweet then why not go in for sweet stuffs like honey, sugar, Fanta, Pepsi, etc. You see, to the outsider certain acts seem stupid and baseless. It is the same with the mission of Christ on earth many years ago. What would force somebody to get up and say he was facing death when he could have run away from it? Not accidental death. But a revealed tormenting painful death. To some, it is mere baseless and has no value. To them it does not pay at all. But to Christ, and for that matter God, there is a very good reason. That is, to redeem us from the clutches of eternal damnation and qualify us for His eternal redemption. To destroy the works of the devil and deliver us from the evils of this world we live in. It is for all these that Christ paid that price with His life (1 John 3:8/ Galatians 1: 4/Colossians1:12):

So, while somebody might have cause for taking in alcohol, God has a much more purpose to cause Christ die for mankind. It is an act that has genuine cause. Don't underrate it. I am bringing this message this afternoon with a very heavy heart. I have just chanced upon a parting gift my late younger brother gave to me some years back. Did he have time to accept Christ as His SacrificedSavior? Shamefully, I can't tell.

Mr. Ecclesiastes, Ghana Says You Are Wrong.

- In the past when our fathers married more than one, there was unity and peace in the households.
- When we had few churches, there was trust and faithfulness.
- When we had little formal education, there was virtually no corruption and selfishness.
- When we had dwarfs, sea goddesses and ancestral spirits, there was truth and obedience.
- When we had mud school buildings, no electricity and computers, there was respect and humility among the youth.
- When our young girls and mothers went about in modest dressings, there was godliness and fear of God in sexual cravings.
- When there was no premium on titles, there was patriotism, accountability and no abuse of office.
- When chiefs/kings displayed selfesteem, our young girls were not taken advantage of.

The writer of Ecclesiastes 7:10 once said to the effect that we should never say the former days were better than now. But I am convinced if he were to be in Ghana today, he'd withdraw his statement. So, Mr. Ecclesiastes, Ghana is saying you are wrong! Bam!

The Gem in the Sand: Thankfulness in the Face of Challenges.

Kindly allow me to give this personal testimony. It's a personal life experience which might serve for our faith in God. Most often we feel overtly ashamed of the negative situations we find ourselves in, like the man born blind that Jesus healed, we don't want friends, church members, relatives, coworkers, neighbors point at us and say, "Is this not the man who used to..." (John 9:8&9). But that is when we are to remain calm in our faith. God would reveal His secret shaping of our lives including those connected to us. My (now) 21yearold daughter and 26yearold nephew have lived with me all these years. My daughter has just completed KNUST recently and is about to do her National Service whilst my nephew finished his graduation and National Service last year. I sometimes wonder why they never go out even free times to have fun as I used to do especially when I dropped out of the seminary; disco dancing, partying, boozing, street fighting, etc. Often times, I'd call and try to advise them about dating. And they'd politely tell me they have great purpose in life and what I am thinking is not what their focus in life is. They want live good moral life and achieve something great in life.

My daughter for the past three weeks has been commuting between Accra and Kumasi following on her National Service posting. But the past 4 days she has had to perch with another coursemate of hers and the family in Accra so that she could be a little stressfree. Both of them belong to the youth missionary unit of their fellowship. Yesterday, she called me from Accra. She has been posted to the Sogakope branch of the Ghana Commercial Bank (GCB) in the Volta region for her National Service. So, she called and asked for Ghc 25 (equivalent of US$5.67 or £4.39). What would this do? "Daddy, don't worry. I know the challenges you are facing now. I'll manage. Maybe I can take shortshort." That was her response. Tears flowed from my eyes. I, Joe Adus, of all people? Why these challenges, Lord?

Then the Holy Spirit opened my ears and heart, "Why complain and weep? So, can't you read through? You are thinking of your status. But can't you see the positive moulding God is doing in her life? How many young ladies of her age would still be depending on their parents? There are girls of her age who are 'independent' because they have the means through immoral lifestyle. Under graduates and graduates who are not asking for Ghc25 (US$ 5.67/£4.39) but they have sold out their lives. If your daughter is asking for this amount, don't worry about your fame. Rather be thankful to the Lord for shaping her to suit His call as a young missionary."

That's the point. Yes, the situation may be embarrassing. But let's allow God to work through us for the edification of His Name, that God might be glorified in such embarrassing situations/challenges (John 9:3).

A Dog Called "Obofuor" (Angel)

I have this dog that I have named 'Obofuor'(i.e. angel). When I first brought him in as a puppy, I'd cuddle him, soothe him, and feed him more than necessary. I pampered him. But as it was growing up, I realized he was not doing what I expected of him. I simply wanted him to be barking especially when a new face came to the house. So, I decided on a strategy. I now put him in chains 24hrs/day and expose him to the sun or when raining. I even whip him several times whilst in chains with a bunch of broom getting him angry and aggressive. I also feed him just once whilst feeding the other pet, the cat called 'Fire' about three times. I make sure 'Obofuor' sees me feed the cat. (Call these Ninja Training.) Now, he has started barking even when he hears the sound of any movement outside the house. This is what I want of him.

In like manner sometimes, God purposefully allows us to get deprived of all sorts of privileges that we might have enjoyed. He sees us chained to unemployment, financial crises, even thrown out of residence due to rent defaulting, sacked from jobs, failed in exams, imprisoned, etc. We get chained whilst we see our colleagues let loosed. We see our friends built houses, whilst we get thrown out; they get awards whilst we get criticized for being irresponsible, etc. These happen not because witches/wizards are attacking us, not because we are irresponsible or lazy, not because we have committed any sin or crime. It is just because God wants us to be what He wants us to be for Him. For the future, for His purpose, and for us. That's why He says even in fire and in the rain, He'd be there for us. (Isaiah 43:2).

Fr. Dorr's 'Son'.

A young slim dark complexion lad of about 12 years. 1977. Bushy hair in the hey days of Kool & the Gang, The Jackson 5, Boney M. I remember very vividly my late mother seeing me off at the Kumasi Kejetia lorry station to Offinso to be under the tutelage of Fr. Dorr CSSp to be trained to become a Catholic Priest, eventually becoming a helping force in the formation and growth of the West Africa Foundation of the Holy Ghost Congregation/ Frs. It was something like Samuel's mother sending him to serve under Eli (1 Samuel 1:2428). At Offinso, I was the attention of all wherever I happened to be. Fr. Dorr's son. Not in the biological sense though. As a mission boy, I was also the toast of most of the young guys, both males and females alike. Whenever I passed by the children would remark, "Fr. Dorr's son". I felt good. What a privilege! A mission boy under Fr. Dorr. Not just a mission boy but somebody under the care of a priest. Not only an ordinary priest but a Catholic priest, wellrespected. Not only any Catholic priest, but a white man. I loved the attention I attracted. And I enjoyed it.

Then one day, the first time I served at the Mass, I messed myself up. I never cared to study and practice serving Mass service like the other Mass Servers. After all, I was Fr. Dorr's 'son'. But when it mattered most, I messed up. Those of you who know the Order of the Mass understand how every move is well and methodically structured: when to knee, stand up, bow down, carry the Bible, throw the incense, carry the Cross and lead the procession. All these I never bothered to learn and practice. After all I was Fr. Dorr's favorite. On that first day that I served at the Mass, at the St. Agnes Catholic Church at MaaseOffinso, I disgraced myself. Instead of kneeling with the others I'd turn right. Instead of bowing my head, I'd spin around. Instead of bringing the chalice I'd be standing. Everybody saw me disorganizing the service. Shame.

Later in the day, Fr. Dorr summoned me to his office. All he did was to stare at me without saying a word. I knew I had disgraced and disappointed him. There are most us here who claim sonship to God, in fact coheirs with Christ, as believers/Christians/Men of God, etc. But if God were to appear before us in our closet, I am sure we'd bow down our heads in shame, disgraceful disappointing folks whose deeds are far from the profile of the deity of Christ. Are we justified as children of God in our homes, workplaces, neighborhood, civil services, political domains, etc? Do our deeds really justify us to be God/Christ's followers?

The Holy Ghost Congregation: My Pharaoh or My Paul?

When you value yourself within your own estimates, you stand the risk of missing out on your stewardship to God. It is not what we do but how God approves and cherishes our services in His name that matter

God has His own way of using us. It is not how we want Him to use us. Yesterday I mentioned one Fr. Dorr in my message as being my guardian. Incidentally somebody on one of my receiving platforms knew of the said Fr. Dorr but didn't know I had any link with him. He Watsapp back, "Amazing. So, you were with Fr. Dorr? Do they remember you?" Interesting. Simple question but very profound to me.

Fr. Dorr was the Vocations Director through whom the Congregation of the Holy Ghost (Fathers) was established in Ghana stretching its tentacles to the West African Foundation. That was in 1978. First, gathering of aspirants at Offinso, then the formation at Bantama, to the novitiate and Philosophy at Ejisu, onward. Small beginning but now with priests scattered abroad. Since Fr. Dorr was based at Offinso, it meant the aspirants (all those who wanted to join the Congregation as its trainees) would meet at Offinso from different parts of the country during the long vacations. And as a mission boy with Fr. Dorr and also an aspirant myself, I had to take care of the visiting aspirants. It wasn't easy at all. Apart from my normal chores at the mission house and the church, I also had to find time to cater for my colleague aspirants. I must proudly but with all humanity say, I was the little worm that God used to gather His agents of Ghanaian Holy Ghost Fathers who are now scattered abroad. The likes of.......(Sorry, I can't mention names here.)

Now to the question, "Do they remember you?"

I occasionally get in touch with some of the pioneers. But I dare say, I don't know if I am significant in their daily routines. A case of a new Pharaoh who didn't know Joseph (Exodus 1:8). And for all those who came out later, they are the Abrahams and Israelis who do not acknowledge us (Isaiah 63:16). But should that bother me? No. As Paul said, we are a sacrifice drink being poured out as an offering for the cause of God's service to mankind (Philippians 2 :17). Wherever they are, I wish them well.

OWASS (Akatakyie Boys) and The Holy Communion

In the Catholic Church, in taking the communion you walk SOLEMNLY to the Priest, take it and walk back to your seat in a very seemingly SOLEMN "sanctimonious' mood, very quiet and gentle. I remember one day those of us from the St Hubert Seminary (SAHUSS) attended a program with other selected schools at the Opoku Ware Secondary School (OWASS). We got 'shocked' during communion time. What happened? Whenever the OWASS chaps (aka Akatakyie) went for their communion, their colleagues would give them fans; shouted their names and applauded. For example,

- "Joooooooooooe Adus".
- "Wakiiiiiiiiiki".
- "Mafioso Wataaata Wataaaaatu", etc.

They were having a nice fun. For some of us, sanctimonious prieststobe, it was out of order. Many years after that incident, I am asking myself, why 'condemn' the Akatakyie lads? Weren't they more frank than some of us who were putting up the air of piety just because that is/was what the system wants(ed) us to put up? Moreover, why should they not have fun/happy in the presence of God? Most of us are in the house of God yet far from

JOE ADUSEI

inner joy because of not what we are but because of pretence and hypocrisy. We pretend to be just to please the system but not who and/or what we truly are. If only we could be free, open, and true with ourselves without any pretence and hypocrisy. Kudos to you, my Akatakyie brothers.

Scenes of Austria And the Grace of God

I often hear of such a statement like,

- "Soandso person could not manage his/her fame.",
- "That poor girl did not manage her stardom that's what killed her",
- "How tragic to see such a promising young chap dead because he did not manage himself well", etc.

Most often I 'insult' myself for apparently throwing away the numerous opportunities that came my way. But to be frank, I ironically dare say I made the best out of all these to be the proud responsible husband and parent I could be, something which my family themselves pride themselves with. *"Our father is the most responsible parent in the world"*, my children like almost all children who adore their parents, would say. And not only my family but some outsiders as well. Of course, my other side of lifestyle may also give its own verdict. Well despite such sense of responsibility, I am sometimes tempted to give in to the concerns over material gains; money, buildings, cars, high profiledpositions, etc. For instance, sometimes, I find my other sense questioning me,

- *"Joe, what do you have to show for all the foreign trips/ locations you had the privilege to embark on the past?"*
- *"Don't you think God opened all these doors for you, but you could not take the opportunity to establish yourself?*

Austria, Egypt, France, UK, Italy, Switzerland, Netherlands, Kenya, Benin, Togo, Nigeria, Germany, (almost all the States in the) US, La Cote d'Ivoire, etc.

- *"What benefits did you gain from them?"*,
- *"Where are the connections you made? What are the gains you made from them?"*
- *"You failed to exploit and handle them."*

That is my inner sense sometimes battling with my moral. But how do we define the failure, the mismanagement, the lost opportunities, etc? Do you blame yourself because your choice of wealth does not reflect somebody's lifestyle or wealth? As I sit right now watching a movie on Go TV Movie Zone channel 103, the setting of which is in Austria, my mind goes down the memory how in 1999 I travelled to and walked along the same streets of Vienna which I am seeing right now in the movie. It was just a fourday trip. But I still remember the ancient landscape of that historical city.

Yes, there are a lot of young promising lads who might have lost their lives because, as we often hear, *"they could not manage their fame and wealth"*. But the most important thing is not losing out or not managing your wealth/opportunities/fame, etc. What matters is, as Caleb told Joshua in the Bible, "it is the grace of God that has kept me alive all these years". (Joshua 14:710). God has kept you alive because His grace .and blessings are still upon you, a sure sign that He has made you a blessing to yourself and others. (Isaiah 65:8). Find out how you can be of help to others more than what you want to be for yourself. Remember the words of Habakkuk 3: 17 & 18,

Though the fig tree does not blossom, nor fruit be on the vines, the produce of the olive fails, and the fields yield no food, yet I will rejoice in the God of my salvation.

The Vandal Crown but Not Vandalistic Character

When filling the admission forms for entry into the University in 1983, I only knew of Legon and Akuafo Halls of residence. I never knew of Commonwealth Hall. So, I didn't choose that Hall. But either by divine grace or work of the oracles, I was posted to Commonwealth Hall which automatically made me a "Vandal". And I would have regretted if it hadn't been so because the Hall gave me the lifestyle I stood for. Members of that Hall are referred to as *Vandals*. We proudly accept this accolade not because of what others think of ours as being nuisance but what we understand and accept to be the ideals of a V. A. N. D. A. L.:

- 'V' for Vivacious.
- 'A' for Altruistic.
- 'N' for Neighborly.
- 'D' for Devoted.
- 'A' for Affable.
- 'L' for Loyal.

Late last night, I was unexpectedly rushed to the hospital for very severe stomach upset and headache. One of the elderly nurses on duty gave me an exceptional service upon learning from conversation that I am an old Vandal. She explained to me her late husband was a Vandal. Amazing. Oh so, we are not all that a bad reference to the vandalistic character but rather a crown of dignity and respect eh?

There was a time when Jesus in His ministry was discredited, *"Is this not the carpenter?"* (Mark 6:3). But He didn't allow this to sway Him from His mission. Most often, we give in too much to what people think of, see and say of us. We give in, get discouraged and fall back. No. Know who you are and capable of doing and keep going. Your success lies not in the measure of others but in the **Will** of God, more so what God has made you but not what others but think of you. I wear the "Vandal crown" but won't be discouraged by what others see as the "vandalistic character" in me. Thank you, Aunty Maggie and your team for your exceptional service to me last night. Have a good weekend.

Room B10, Commonwealth Hall and the Case of Paul

In 1989, my final year at the University of Ghana, I had a personal dramatic experience with the Spirit of God similar to that of Apostle Paul's encounter in Acts 9:118. It happened right in my room in B10 in the "almighty" Commonwealth Hall. It was an encounter which, one would be tempted to say, should have seen me become one of the globally known preachers of Christ by now, perhaps in the same vein of the ministries of the likes of Apostle Paul himself, A.A. Allen, Kathryn Kuhlman, Mother Theresa, Billy Graham, W. J. Kumuyi, Annor Yeboah, etc. But the focus is not on me in this message. It is on the apostle Paul and God's own tool of purpose. And this is where we fail as Christians especially socalled anointed Men of God. Imagine being called and anointed by God. Imagine being blessed with whatever blessings you need. Imagine demonstrating all sense and commitment to your fellow being. Then despite all these you find yourself under "any attack" both physically and spiritually. This is the very thing Paul orchestrated against the early church (Acts 9:1&2). Paul's persecution was not based on the theology/zeal of Judaism alone but was also vested in the spiritual ventures of his time. So apart from physical attack he was in some way powered by a spiritual force, if it were to be in our time, we'd say satanic/demonic powers.

But in all this, God had His own way of handling him and his attacks. He weaved Paul and his persecution of the church, into a network of bringing people to His call for salvation through Christ and increasing His sheepfold (Acts 9:2631). Christianity has now become a tool of sending down consuming fire to burn into ashes our "enemies". We claim, as Men of God to have powers to let those who work against our church members go mad.

As claimed Men of God, we publicly boast of the anointing to turn into snakes and bite to kill those we consider to be attacking us. As Christians, we are always seeking directives to eliminate those we consider to be working against. We heap cools of judgmental fire on our work place supervisors when they correct us for our shortcomings. Why? Why? Why? Why do we always have to be praying to destroy our perceived enemies/persecutors/attackers? Instead of living a lifestyle of winning souls, we seem to occupy ourselves with issues which can only be handled by God. And that's why I wish all those of us, especially those who have the bigger platforms; big churches, TV stations, radio broadcast facilities, etc. would stop this "destroytheenemy" syndrome and let God work His own way out in our lives.

In the Football boots of Barcelona FC

I like football/soccer. And I like the excitement that goes with it. I once played briefly for Anokye Stars, the junior team of Asante Kotoko, in the early 80s. I was once a ball boy, standing on the touchlines and collecting the ball when it went off the line. My favorite players include Anthony Yeboah, Sulley Muntari, John Painstill, C Ronaldo, Xavi, Lampard, and John Terry. My favorite team? I don't have any specific one. Rather I tend to follow any team that Jose Mourinho goes to as a coach though Holland is my favorite team. Despite this interest, I always find it absolutely boring and time wasting when a 'bigger' team plays a 'lesser' one. For instance, I find most games involving Barcelona FC irritating. Not because I hate them. They are too good and of greater quality than most of the teams. So, you see them always dominating and scoring goals more than necessary. So, I tend to ignore watching their games. I won't waste my time on them because they'd win.

The Bible tells us that God is far greater than agents and challenges working against us. By my faith therefore I won't waste my time focusing on the socalled devil and his works. I don't worry about the challenges not because I am irresponsible and a careless chap. I'd try to work toward solving my challenges, but I simply won't waste my time always brooding over them. I am always convinced that I'll always win. And truly with God as my focus, victory falls in my basket.

Stupid Diplomats Under Abuja Street Lights

I can't help laughing as I think of it and relive the incident. Somewhere in 2008. I was with the UNDP as the UNV Program Officer doubling also as the UNDP Focal Person on the Avian Influenza in Abuja, Nigeria. Let me take this opportunity to salute (my) UN Resident Representative then, Mr. Albert Kacou. I was also doing my parttime Bible School course in Ministry Management at the Dunamis School of Ministry (DUSOM), under Rev. Dr. Paul Enenche. I salute you too, Dr. Paul. Two hectic schedules at the same time. I also enjoyed driving in the night under the beautiful streets' lights of Abuja. So sometimes I ventured out in the night. Oh, I loved the place. And the friends I made there.

On this particular night, after our occasional treat of French fries and grilled fish at "Abacha Barracks" spot on the AbujaMaraba road, with my office Associate, Lena, I decided to probe further in the night with my lady cotenant and another male friend. I was driving my Honda Concerto which had my assigned UN number plate. (Diplomatic status). We drove to one of the open gardens, came out of the car. My male friend went in to get some drinks whilst I leaned on the back bonnet with my lady cotenant sitting on it beside me chatting. That place was also a popular spot for commercial sex workers. My parking light was on, so you could easily see my number plate. As we chatted, I felt a stroke behind my back 'whip whip' and *"Stupid. Stupid diplomats. You think you can come here and misbehave with our women? Stupid. Stupid."* Two police patrol men. I tried to explain myself, but they said I and the lady were openflirting. To avoid further embarrassment and trouble, we drove out without even calling our male partner. Stupid diplomat in an unacceptable act. Justification for trouble.

You see some of us, I even dare say most of us who claim to be Christians behave as such. We give ourselves all sorts of Christlike tags:

- More than conquerors,
- Touch not my anointed,
- The head not the tail,
- Divinely protected,
- "Apostle Bishop",
- General Overseer,
- The Flying Prophet, etc.

But our lifestyles and deeds tend to betray us. We are more of the stupid diplomats in God's field: pride, jealousy, exploitation, greed, selfishness, jealousy, etc. As for fornication and alcohol, don't let me mention it. Whom are we deceiving? Stupid diplomats in the eyes of God indeed.

The Drumbeats of KKD

Some of you may remember. In the late 80s, there was this popular TV advert by the Ghanaian ace DJ and broadcaster KKD (Kwasi Kyei Darkwah). I have forgotten exactly what the product was. But the clip had some ladies passing by with KKD looking and admiring them. Then he said, "Momma yenka. Ghana maa ho efe" (Let's be frank, Ghanaian ladies are indeed pretty/attractive.). Hmmm.

The other day, I too stood by the main gate of the (Agogo Atonsu) government hospital in Kumasi. I was not sick. I was rather waiting for a friend from Kuntanase. And that was our meeting point. In the course of the waiting, I found myself being attracted to a situation. My eyes started 'admiring' the attractive ladies going in and out of the hospital. They were hospital staff, visitors, and patients. Then one thought came to my mind; this indeed is an appropriate point to get a lady, a 'munching' partner. Sure.

But another realization also dawned on me. This same point is also the same entry and exit points for the sick and the dead. *"Joe, if you take time and go inside the hospital, you'd not see only the attractive ladies you admire. You'd also see dead people, the badly injured and the suffering ".* Two sides of the coin. The same point of attraction is equally the same point of death. That is one of the complex natures of our mortal life which we need to handle with care. The same (desire of) money we enjoy could become the same means of destruction. The same power at our disposal could be the same tool of our downfall. The same sex we enjoy could be the same channel for our sicknesses/diseases/death. The Bible talks of a way that seems right to man but its end is the way to death (Proverbs 14:12). Marriage is divine, but a wrong choice can produce a disaster. Let's be careful in all our endeavors, to watch before we leap.

The Little Elephants in the Jungle of St. Louis

I don't know if my colleagues would remember. I was one of 5 males given the experimental chance to have our Sixth Form "A" Level course at the allgirls St. Louis Sec. School in Kumasi(198284); Dr. Nutakor, (ex)Rev. Fr. Stephen OwusuAfreh, Messrs. Aziz, OkyereBona and myself to mingle with and be psychologically and academically 'tormented' by the likes of Juliana AfumwaaBruce, Vic BoakyeAgyemang, Carol Ackim, Carol Kuffour, Mercy Osei Bonsu, Theo A, Bridget Zato, Fleshy T, J. AddaiAboagye, Cynthia Kankam, Elizabeth B., Felidaps, Ama Sheila(I better shut my mouth), etc. One of our Masters/Tutors, an Irish, Rev. Sister on one occasion referred to us as "Little Elephants". I can't remember exactly what the incidence was. In any case, that's the tag she gave to us.

Did she mean to insult us? Or we were being nuisance to her class? Children can be very disturbing depending on the situation/occasion. On the bus from Kumasi to my hometown yesterday afternoon, there was this child about 5 years old who was crying, yelling and fidgeting here and there. Her father was apparently taking her to somewhere, but she was yelling to "meko me Maame ho"(I want to be with my mother). She was a 'nuisance'; shrieking and yelling, kicking her legs here and there like an excited male horse on heat. I then understood why the apostles of Jesus tried to prevent the little children from going to Him Matthew 19:1315). Little elephants 'disturbing' peace. We are daily or occasionally faced with challenges that are more nuisance than of peace. Everyday worries that disturb our peace; light/water bills, rent, daily bread, debts, etc. Whilst we see them as insurmountable challenges, threatening little elephants in our lives, Jesus says we should bring all such burdens to Him. (Matthew 11:28/Psalm 55:22/1 Peter 5:7). He who carried our eternal damnation on the Cross, can't He solve less tormenting issues?

The Captured Promise by the Pine Trees of Aburi Botanical Gardens

We were very close. Brotherly friends like David and Jonathan in the Bible. Our friendship amazed our other colleagues. Two different personalities/characters from different backgrounds yet bound by an inherent link of friendship. Whenever people sought for him, they would often ask me. But now, we have lost touch, almost ten years now, if I am not mistaken. Yesterday, an old friend of ours met and asked me of this DavidcumJonathan friend I am talking about (name withheld for security reasons). He was shocked to learn that we have 'parted' contacts. Incidentally or coincidentally, when I came home yesterday and was going through my old documents, I chanced upon a letter my friend in question wrote to me in 1992 when he was abroad. Why these references? Two main issues.

   a. I remember one time we had gone on a sort of picnic at the Aburi Botanical Gardens in the Eastern Region of Ghana. We talked about our lives and aspirations. I usually use movies to address issues especially Indian movies. This time, my mind went to a scene in **"Sholay"** where Jai (Amitabh Bacchchan) and Veeru (Dharmendra) assured each other that nothing would separate them not even when they get marriage. We too made similar promises at the Aburi Botanical Gardens. But here we are, well, I am, many years down the lane our friendship seems to have hit the rocks. The last time I heard of him was about ten years ago. I know where he is and vice versa BUT due to some reason which is no fault of us, we have not been in contact despite advanced technology. What is my point here? As committed as were at the Gardens, we have breached our promise. Something has separated us. I must say it baffles me whenever I think of him and our friendship. I never thought that he'd avoid me. But this is where the words of Paul come in (Romans 8: 3539) "…what will separate us from the love of God, neither angels nor rulers, nor height, etc." In the midst of our challenges and afflictions, abundance and lack, acceptance and rejection, a time would come when we'd be left alone. The only companion worth sticking to would be Christ even in eternity. So why not court His friendship!

b. I referred to a letter this friend wrote to me some years ago. In those days such media like email, WhatsApp, Instagram, etc. were not common or in existence. So, the letter was written on what we used to call airmail. It was dated precisely 24th October 1992. As part of his message he lamented that, I quote, *"I don't think I am **destined** to be a rich man (*emphasis mine). He wrote those words because he was apparently facing some grave challenges. In the midst of those challenges, he never saw a way out. Today he holds a very high profile international sensitive post with, what I'd say, mouthwatering benefits and an 'untouchable' status, interacting with the high class in the society. I am not trying to expose him. No, far from that. My question is who, but God can determine his/her destiny? The prophet Jeremiah said it all, *"it is not in man* *who directs his steps*". (Jeremiah 10:23) In whatever you do, and wherever you find yourself or plan your socalled future, know that it is only God who can determine who you are and would be. Not your enemies, friends, Men of God, politicians, etc. Only God.

The Mission Boy's Fears

As a young Mass Server and Mission Boy under the late Rev. Fr. Dorr, CSSp, at Offinso, one of the things I dreaded most was to walk across the altar whenever I thought I had gone wayward. Whether preparing the altar for Mass service or cleaning the church, I was scared to death to walk across or around the altar. On the altar we had the tabernacle light by the side of the Holy Communion which represents the Body of Christ and the presence of His angels. I was always scared that God's Presence there would strike me if I misconducted myself.

As Christians, we often quote 2 Kings 6:16 *"Fear not, for those with us are more than those with them"*, to boast of our trust in God's defencepresence of fiery angels protecting us. So, we fear no evil/orchestration against us.

- But do we sit down to think that those angels/the eyes of God put at our care also see everything we do openly and secretly?
- That when we secretly fornicate with other people's mistresses/husbands, they see?
- That when we alter contract documents they see? That when we think we are smart outwitting others, they see?
- That when as Men of God we seek juju and other ungodly means to operate, they see it? Etc.

I rest my case!

The Tears of My Broken Palm Wine Calabash

In the days of the early church, the name of God/Jesus was held with great honor and fear. In the book of Acts 19:1117, the seven brothers of a Jewish High Priest named Sceva, were beaten up by a demonpossessed man when they tried to cast the evil spirit away by using Jesus' name. In twisting this story, I dare say the evil spirits in our days; demons, and deities which we consider satanic, are all weeping. They are not laughing at us but shedding tears. The likes of Antoa, Patange, Akonodi, Kwaku Bonsam (shrines in Ghana whom we consider satanic/demonic) are weeping. Not because we engage them in spiritual warfare with Holy Ghost 'fire'. They are themselves crying for/over the mockery we, in the name of Christianity, are making of God/Jesus.

Just sit down and think of teachings going on, prophetic directives and 'crazy' stuff by 'Men of God', abuse of the faith of believers, 'bring used panties to church', believers made to crawl when commanded 'my sheep follow me', etc. Oh no, no, no. I tell you my brother/sister, the broken pieces of the calabash I used to drink palm wine from is crying. Not because I stopped taking palm wine but that the NAME of God is being dragged to the dust.

The Cassock of Piesie and the Boxing Gloves of Mohammed Ali

The book of Ezekiel 34 talks strongly against the leaders who feed fat on the people. Very strong words from God. But who is to blame? Aren't we the people who have allowed them to feed fat on us? Glamorous clothing, expensive cars, high class restaurants, bootlicking respect, etc. Why blame them? Wait. Who wouldn't enjoy such privileges if you were in their shoes? Would you be bold to reject such 'privileges'? I don't know if my 'brother', Kwame Piesie, remember this incidence. I had then left the seminary. He was then an already ordained priest. He came to our house at Abrepo junction, opposite the Philips Commercial School. My late mother was still sad I had left the catholic priesthood. After 'cooling down' my mother, he drove me to Nkawie. And he broke the news to me. He was going to resign from the priesthood. Whaat! An already accomplished, academic scholar, very popular, respected, an influential priest! Why resign and lose all the privileges that come with the priesthood? And why tell me, your minor even before breaking the news officially to the church's hierarchy? We were later to drive to the Bishop's house at Dakwadwam, near the TUC quarters where he boldly tendered in his resignation.

This incidence has since endeared him to me. He perceived there was something wrong and he would not compromise it. The late great boxing legend, late Mohammed Ali, is said to have, at a point in time, boldly thrown away his heavyweight title belt and allowed himself to be stripped of the title for refusing to join the US army to go and fight in Vietnam. He too perceived there was something wrong with the system and he was not prepared to compromise. The privileges of wearing the cassock and the boxing gloves voluntarily rejected out of the sense of integrity by these two men I have mentioned.

Privileges enjoyed have often led to the continuous abuse of the system because those who would have led to its correction tend to shut up instead of shouting. There is something seriously wrong with/in the church, civil service, presidency, judiciary, academia, etc. Is somebody out there who is prepared to 'remove his cassock or throw his gloves into the bin"? Titles, public recognition, popularity, diplomatic status, etc.

First Class Flight from Gilgal to Jordan

When Elijah was to be taken up to heaven, he was accompanied by Elisha from Gilgal to the overshores of Jordan. Upon reaching the banks of river Jordan, Elijah struck the river with his cloak which opened up and they crossed over. (2 Kings 2:18). After his master had been taken up, Elisha was to return to base. This time the Jordan had closed up again. God knew Elisha would return. But why didn't He wait till Elijah had crossed over before closing it up again? Why waited till after Elisha had struck it before opening it again for him to cross over? This means life depends primarily on you yourself, your own choices, intuition, initiatives, skills, experiences, understanding. It is unfortunate that we mostly have to live according to the dictates of others. We throw away our culture because others say it is substandard and demonic. We dress according to dictates of others, food, language, marriage, education, etc. This is sadder for those of us Christians. We allow ourselves to be brainwashed and exploited by socalled Men of God/Priests/Pastors. Christianity is more of your own personal relationship with God. Yes, the Bible says (2 Chronicles 20:20) we should believe in His prophets and we shall prosper. But this has often been misused. The Pastor/Priest/Prophets are there to guide us not to manipulate us. We often blame (some of) them for exploiting the church. But it is our own fault. We easily fall prey to them. Because, we give in to whatever they say without us building our own strong stand in the Lord. We jump at their antics, the sound of their voices, the popularity of their names and titles, the population of their churches, etc. without reading deep into what should have been the substance of what they say they are. Note well what Elisha said, "Where is **the Lord, God** of my father Elijah?"(2 Kings 2:14). Not where is my father Elisha or his anointing? It is high time we sat down and developed our own personal intimacy with the God we trust.

My Daughter Lydia, King Herod and Anas Aremeyaw Anas

- Lydia is my daughter whom I named after my (foster) mother, Maa Lydia, the former and first Ghanaian headmistress of St. Louis Senior High School.
- King Herod was the King in charge of the Jewish state during the days of John the Baptist and Jesus.
- Anas Aremeyaw Anas is a Ghanaian international investigative journalist whose works have roared a lot of storm in the society.
    This is Just a brief introduction.
- Catholics today June 24th commemorate the Feast of John the Baptist in recognition of his significant role in the salvation process of mankind through Christ. John the Baptist is commemorated twice in the Catholic calendar, June 24th (his birth) and August 29th (his death). It is the role and mission of this messenger of God that have prompted this message today. Not long ago my daughter Lydia got the opportunity to embark on an educational trip abroad with some other youth. The host institution

offered to foot the bill of internal expenses whilst there. All she needed was the air ticket and pocket money. (I am giving these details to raise a point). To some, this was a very big problem in monetary times. But to those who have the abundance of money, it wasn't a big issue. So, she approached a lot of people to solicit 'sponsorship'. Unacceptably but as usual, almost all the men she approached sought to sleep with her. Some of them were even people who know me very well and vice versa. And unknown to them, all these attempts she reported back, every one of them. A way of saying *"be perished with your money"*. It is not every commodity that can be bought with money. I'd say I am not surprised because I know who she IS. (So, if you are reading me and are one of such persons, note that I am already aware of your move. She is not Anas, but you are exposed). Though not surprised by these moves because it has become the other of the day, there is one of them who has kept me thinking. A wellknown PARAMOUNT Chief. Mention him and even an ant can point to who he is. Hmm. (As for him, if he is hearing me, I stand in the presence of God and declare the end of his reign. The whole world will hear of his fall.)

- In the book of Matthew 14:112, King Herod in other to please his illegitimate stepdaughter on his birthday, had John the Baptist killed and his head offered as a gift to her. Gift of evil. Gift of doom. Gift of deceit and destruction perpetuated from the throne of authority.

I am not worried because it attempted my daughter. I am worried because there are many vulnerable girls out there who are daily being exploited, abused, and victimised just because they cannot stand on their feet. There are many people out there who give in because their 'oppressors' are 'King Herod' the powerful voice, the person of status quo. It does not affect only women but even men as well; not only individuals but entire communities as well. We are in a society where reason has been thrown into the den of beasts. Humanity has been pushed from the right path, and inhuman doctrines and policies put in place to determine our fate. No one can trust his neighbor any more. People laugh at you with open teeth but in the depth of their hearts, there is a hidden dagger of destruction. Is this the society we want? Nanka Bruce, Muyiwa and Fr. Tony Kwasi Appiah, Lydia appreciates you for coming to her aid.

The Voice of John the Baptist or the Uplifting of Satan?

I often ask myself, what's the point in 'preaching' the gospel? Haven't people of old, prophets, preachers, etc. done so? Has that changed the society? Or is it that those of us who claim we have been called by God, have mispresented the divine reality? This leads to the question "are we preaching the gospel of Christ at all as commissioned in the great commission? (Matthew 28:19&20). I dare say NO. The other day, a pastor friend visited me, and we picked up this discourse. He ascertained that the gospel has now been preached to every part of the world and that might hasten the 2nd coming of Christ. No way. In as much as I can't challenge the 2nd coming of Christ, I dare say the gospel has not been preached to the ends of the world. What we claim to be the gospel going around is not the gospel. The pulpit is worse than when Jesus drove out from the synagogue those turning it into a business venture (John 2: 1316). Don't tell me what is happening in so called churches is the voice of John the Baptist heralding the kingdom of God. The church and what's happening are manifestations of Satan pointing to us the riches of the world thereby deceiving us: big churches and multitude of congregations, prosperity gospel, famous titles, great followers, misplaced prophetic unction, selfexultation of socalled men of

God with rabbinic appearances, false but polished doctrines, etc. No. The end of the world may be drawing near but not because the 'gospel' is preached. Rather, the gospel is pushed away from our daily paths. Don't blame Satan. If we have decided to follow his bait, don't let us pretend we are against him. He is winning.

The Sacred Mantle of Hotep Ra: Blessings for Us but Not Others?

The Hotep Ra dynasty of ancient Egypt, which sanctioned the powers of Pharaohs, gave in when a (Hebrew) slave, Joseph, from a foreign land was appointed the second most powerful authority in Egypt, subject to Pharaoh only. (Genesis 41:157). This elevation of Joseph is seen as one of the unique graces, favors, love and upliftment of God towards His faithful. So, in our times, we (mostly Christians) look up to experiencing this great feat of Joseph: fasting, prayers, prophetic gathering, anointing and impartation services, seed sowing, crusades, etc. We want God to elevate us even as He did to Joseph in a 'foreign land'.

This is where I find it absurd. Aren't we the same people who oppose government's appointees because the person is not from our community/district/region or even our political party? Aren't we the same people who object to and work against people assuming positions of importance among us because they are not from our tribes/ethnic? We oppose others from marrying into our families. We despise others because they are not up to our social status, religion, academic feats, and professional groups. Even in our Christian classification, we look down on those who are not of the same denominations with us. As Men of God, we see ourselves as more anointed to the extent that we sometimes despise others whom we feel are not up to the level of our anointing.

We want to be elevated and appreciated elsewhere like Joseph. But we don't want others to be elevated among us. What then is the use of all the church buildings, the crusades, prophetic convocations, societal meetings, anointing/impartation services if at the end of the day we produce people who only look into themselves because they see themselves as "a chosen race...God's own people..."(1 Peter 2:9)? Hypocrisy at the highest level!

The Gods Turning Around in a Musical Chair?

When we were (well, when I was) growing up, and from our traditional background, we developed keen interest in such entities like dwarfs, the river gods, Maame Water (Marine Spirit Head), ancestral spirits. Stories about them were friendlier and positively oriented as entities that manifested in helping people. They became angry only after being offended. Dwarfs would 'kidnap' a person and empower him to come home and help the community with the acquired spiritual powers. The river god of a particular enclave made sure sanity prevailed in his enclave. Our ancestral spirits would manifest and sometimes lead a person to unearth hidden gold treasures. These were the norm of the day.

And now modern Christian interpretations have turned the tide round. Almost in every Christian program, especially prophetic programs, you hear of dwarfs spiritually stealing somebody's money as being the cause of the person's financial crisis. You hear of marine spirits spiritual marrying somebody as being the cause of the person's marital challenges, and even his general wellbeing as well. You hear of ancestral altars being the cause of a family's downfall.

My question is what went wrong that all these entities have now become the offenders instead of the goodwill they represented in the society? Is it a case of misplaced conceptualization by modern day Christians? Is it myopic and blind ideologies which have turned against these traditional beliefs, and which we have blindly swallowed up? Is it because what we took to exist in the past never existed but were mere fairy tales? If so, what about modernday prophetic interpretations? Are they also mere deceiving fabrications? If really these entities exist(ed), since when did they become evil instead of the goodwill they represented in the society? And what was the cause? Are we using Christianity to establish a notion which does not exist? How well do we justify, or discredit our Christian ideologies in the face of such alarming questions?

Why Should I Vote for a President?

Some years back when I heard that exPresident John Mahama was an old Vandal and a section of the populace condemning him/his government, I felt ashamed and offended. Ashamed because I felt he had disappointed the Vandal/Commonwealth Hall fraternity. And offended because I felt he had the right to embark on whatever policies he wanted to implement. At the end of it all I questioned myself why should I bother myself to go and queue in the stand to vote for somebody as a President who may not care about how I wake up and struggle all day to even buy my little baby a tin of milk? What about those who go all out to defend and demonstrate their loyalty to a President. Here I am talking of all presidents as well as those in influential positions. The answer is, those who hold their allegiance definitely get some benefits from the 'President'. So, Joe, if you don't, they know what they get so better shut up. *Na so oooo.*

It is the same for those of us who claim to be believers in God/Christ. When others sneer at us for being believers, we don't have to fight back. We need not insult them. It is up to us to focus and demonstrate our loyalty to (the) God/Christ we claim to hold in high esteem. Our challenge is to prove to them what sort of benefits we get from our belief and trust. And this can only be done when we actually prove our loyalty with the sincere discipline and lifestyles befitting a believer/Christian, the same way the early church was first christened "Christians" in Antioch by their lifestyle (Acts 11:2226).

Sailing in The KBL Ship and Swallowing the Unswallowable

I remember some years back. I was then doing my Masters at the KNUST. On this particular day, I joined my colleagues from Unity Hall on an excursion trip to the then Kumasi Brewery Ltd (KBL), brewers of beer at Ahinsan, Kumasi. Surely, we knew we'd have a taste of beer once we got in. But some of us, 'foolishly' decided to go in for the highly alcoholic local stuff, akpeteshie(apio), before entering the brewery. I remember C Boray was one of us. Can somebody tell me where he is now? Long time. Anyway. That day, the 'amateurs' among us could not stand it. They kept on vomiting over and over and over. My 'expertise' in past alcoholic exploits has taught me that, no matter how good and experienced you are in consuming alcohol, there are certain alcoholic beverages you dare not combine or even take alone in great quantities. If you dare, you'd vomit and make a mess out of yourself. The apostle Paul had a great concern for the Thessalonians. They were some of the people he dedicated much of his ministry to, writing the first and second books of Thessalonians. To this, they in turn responded with great respect. They would thus not challenge the status and any word that came out of Paul's mouth. They appeared to just swallow whatever Paul said. But the less fancied people of Berea were not like that. Call them nonentities but they would not swallow anything that came out just because Paul and co were apostles. The Bereans listened to Paul and co, but they would not fool themselves by swallowing whatever they were told (Acts 17:10 & 11).

The other way appears to be the tragedy of our society now, swallowing any word that comes to us: from the church, politics, academia, sports, business, etc. We tend to quickly swallow anything we hear without any calculated effort of examining them. In the end we allow ourselves to be pushed into a "onecorner" calamity without any way out. Let's be Bereans and save ourselves instead of swallowing up crazy stuffs that have the potential of leading us into the filthy gutters of vomiting.

The Mystery of Okomfo Anokye and The Reality of Jesus Christ.

Doreen, my sisterinlaw was visiting us in Kumasi from Takoradi. On this particular day I took her to the Komfo Anokye Teaching Hospital where the legendary Komfo Anokye Sword is placed as a tourist attraction. History has it that the legendary traditional priest, Komfo Anokye, who lived in the 17th century, just let go the sword from his hands on the ground and up till now no one has been able to 'uproot' it from the ground where it is now still. It is reported that this happened somewhere in 1667, about 350 years ago. Remember, it is this same person who commanded the Golden Stool from the sky and caused it to be one of the greatness of the Asante nation/people.

At the site, we listened to the narrative of the guide with keen interest. History indeed is exciting. Back home later in the evening I began to relive the guide's account of this person who is said to be one of the greatest fetish priests ever to have lived. Then I started asking myself, why do people believe such a figure but doubt the reality of Jesus Christ? Why do we believe in the exploits of such figures like Kwame Nkrumah, Marcus Garvey, Othman dan Fodio, Jaja Opobo, Sundiata, Hannibal, Alexander the Great, Allan Quaterman, Marco Polo, etc. yet are quick to dismiss the life of Jesus; His birth, mission, exploits, etc. We believe in the liberation struggle and conquest of the personalities I have mentioned above. Why the difficulty in believing the messianic mission of Jesus? As somebody said, I can't think far. It doesn't make sense to me.

Trip to My Spiritual Family

The late Bob Marley in his song "No Woman No Cry" remembered some of his past with the lyrics "when we used to sit in the government yard in Trench town". Memories. I too remember how about two and half years ago, I did something 'crazy' in the name of the Lord. I am used to fasting on my own terms. But this time round it seemed crazier. 35 days *dry* fasting. What do I mean by *dry*? No sip of water at all. No bite of any food at all. No taste of any edible piece at all. At some point, there was even no urine or toilet coming from me. I was completely dry. From 12 midnight to 12 midnight. Nothing at all of that sort. And it wasn't like I was at a hideout or at an isolation location. No. I was working at the same time. I was then in charge of a project overseeing two refugee camps of about 13, 000 refugees in all besides project staff. I'd wake up around 3am, do my mediation/prayers, get myself prepared, drive about 2 hours to the camp, get back around 6pm, go to the church to pray, go home to sleep around 9pm, get up again at 3am. And it continued that way. And in all these for 35 days, I never took a sip of water, or any bite of any foodstuff. Does it worth it? Crazy move. I looked more than a caricature. My family, staff, neighbors, superiors, fellowship members all got worried. I am sure some of you may argue if there was any justification for it. Well, it is not you. It is I. I did it not to ask God for food, anointing, favor, money, or any particular breakthrough. I simply termed it *Trip to My Spiritual

Family*. Yes, to relive in myself that God and His agents exist and that they truly work in the affairs of man. (Daniel 4:17). I wasn't proving to anybody but to cherish that idea myself.

It was I and God. Last night, my wife and I during our conversation raised this memory and we laughed over it. What impact, after all this 'crazy' move has it made on my life and those in my life? What impact has it made as far as my relationship with God and His purpose for my life, are concerned? Can I really say I have been living up to God's expectation? After all, said and done, even now or in death, would I have a place in the very heavenly realm I claimed to have visited? Note well, it is not all those who say Lord, Lord will enter the Kingdom of God. (Matthew 7:2123). The time is very short, and the days are evil. Remember, it is appointed unto man to die once, and after that face judgment. (Hebrews 9: 27).

35 days dry fasting, and so what?

That is the question.

I sometimes question myself. In other words, we cannot boast about our socalled exploits in the Lord whilst missing out our place in His kingdom.

For me, all such feats of man as ability to pray, preaching, alms, anointing, healing, deliverance, etc. become useless if they don't 'thy Kingdom come'.

The Succulent Breasts of Mary, the Mother of Christ

There's this song I like much: "Elijah, ma ogya no mmra (Twi: Let the fire come down, Elijah). Prophet Elijah is long gone. Are we invoking his spirit? No. If it were so, then we'd be going against God's decree not to consult mediums. In praying that song, Christians are calling for God's grace/power that He showered on Elijah to also manifest in our lives. It is not Elijah but his God we are addressing. Mary is a key figure among Catholics, but which has also caused controversies/misconceptions for others. Yesterday, I don't know why but, my mind all of sudden got occupied by issues related to her. Unless it is out of ignorance or 'jealousy', Mary is one unique figure in the Bible. I'd even dare say, greater than all the biblical figures except Christ himself. From her teenage up to the day of Pentecost/the formation of the early church, she continued to be a key factor. She is the overall model of motherhood, associated with the shame, challenges, perseverance and fulfillment of Christ mission on earth. Maybe Catholics have not been able to explain their " adoration" for her, but she signifies a lot for humanity: let thy will be done (humility and submission to God); total support for Christ's mission even on the Cross, etc.

This was given meaning and justification when that woman in Luke 11:27 openly declared, *"blessed are the breasts that suckled you"*. With regard to her statue among Catholics, go to most churches now. You'd find their pulpits decorated with the national flags of countries. What has that got to do with Christianity? These flags and the statue of Mary, which has more meaning and significance for Christianity?

I don't blame others for these controversies. May be Catholics themselves have failed to offer sound teachings on these issues to the outside world.

By the way, did you know that a mosque in Abu Dhabi was renamed after Mary *Mariam, Umm Eisa*: Mary, Mother of Jesus, in Abu Dhabi in the UAE? Come, let's go there on a visit.

River Twobiri at KunsuWioso and The Greatness in Life

There is this small tiny river (or is it a stream?) at the outskirts of my hometown, KunsuWioso. It is called "Twobiri". For those of you who may have difficulty, you can pronounce 'Tw' as the 'ch' in 'church'. It is so small that even a toddler can jump over. We cross it before going to the farm on the eastern side. There was an incident when we were children, about 50 years ago. One of my uncles, still alive, by name "The Whole" for his massive strength, had an encounter with and beat up the Police who had just been stationed there to serve the communities around. They were about 4 policemen. He beat them all. Reinforcement was sent in from the twodistrict headquarters of Tepa and Mankranso who stormed the town. People fled. Some to the direction of river Twobiri. The Police chased us up. But when they got to the river, surprisingly it swelled up into a big watercourse. The people crossed over but not the Police. The incident was even published in one of the national dailies, "The Pioneer". Such was the "hidden, unseen, unrecognized" greatness of the small tiny river/stream Twobiri. This incident brings to fore one of the tragedies in life, i.e. despising the 'less' in favor of the 'great'. We tend to overlook the "small" untapped values/greatness in us and people/situations/opportunities/resources in our lives. We look at the greatness and wealth of others and condemn ourselves. We overlook our morals/ethics but copy blindly those of others. We cry and bemoan seeing the upliftment of others in society, their positions, buildings, cars, etc. But we forget that God made Israel out of only Abraham and then barren Sarah. We forget to appreciate that it is out of that small vagina that gives birth to the grownup adult. We forget that the greatest of all beats is not the lion or the elephant but the wisdom of the tiny ant. We fail to appreciate that despite all the big mansions, villas one builds, man would end up in that small 6feet grave. Think over these facts and never condemn yourself.

The Vandals Are Coming

Nobody asked me to do it. I designed it on my own. I loved doing it. And I enjoyed it. We Vandals (students of Commonwealth Hall, University of Ghana) took interest in what was termed "proce". Anytime we felt like registering our interest in any case on campus, we would embark on procession(proce) from our Hall, marched out to wherever we wanted to register our presence, most often to the other Halls of residence; Volta, Akuafo, Legon, Sarbah, etc. And in all this, I'd dress up like a Ninja, hence the accolade "The Vandal Ninja". Those were the days when the rich and the poor, the unbelievers and "chrifes", the city and rural folks all lived as one big family in the Hall. The days of the likes of Joe Wise, Castro, Kesson, Jutta, Joe Mens, Whisky, Buchey, P Shane, Gyamfi, Ammunition, Ecoute, Timo, Ziggy, Adwe, Foster, Sackitey, Banson, Sappiro, Siduu, Pope Feg, Kofi Dennis, Nii Adote, Billy, Kwaitoo, etc. That was somewhere in the 1980s.

This morning I went to one of the Banks to transact some transactions courtesy one of our colleagues. When I stepped out the bank, I saw a couple come out of their flashy Toyota Corolla saloon car. I passed by them. But then the gentleman drew my attention,

"Excuse me. It seems I know you", he said and continued, "You were at Legon"? "Commonwealth Hall?"

Yes.

"I don't remember the name. But you used to dress like a ninja."

I smiled. *"Yes. Joe Adus".*

Then he introduced his wife. He was at Legon Hall and the wife, Volta Hall during my time. The wife recounted the day we (Vandals) invaded Volta Hall in the (US) $2,400 travelers cheque theft incident involving me and my American girlfriends, which led to the famous breakup of the VV (VandalVolta Halls) Alliance somewhere in 1987 or so. What was it? One may ask. It was historic because it was characterized by the suicide attempt and neardeath of a female student from the Volta Hall. Let me tell you briefly what happened. Some US female students were on exchange program on campus. They were five of them. I happened to befriend them at the same time. A week before the incident, I had joined the Dance Department of the School of Performing Arts (SPA) to Cape Coast on a weekly tour. Two days after I returned, in the evening I was going out with the American ladies and we walked through the Legon Hall. I saw people looking at me without any clue as to what was going on. Then the ladies told me. During my absence somebody had entered their room and stole their travelers' cheque amounting to US$ 2,400 (Two Thousand Four Hundred US Dollars). Stories were going around that I had stolen the money. But fortunately, they found out the culprit, a lady from Volta Hall who incidentally happened to be my former girlfriend. Perhaps, she wanted to punish me for dumping her. The US students said they didn't want to tell me at first but at the same time they felt bad because people were still talking about me. So, they now told me. The following day, I took a piece of chalk and wrote in front of our Hal, i.e. C'Wealth Hall, **"KBlock has done it again. US$ 2, 400 stolen by K 'Block Fish. Vandal exonerated". (**Kblock in Volta Hall was where the lady culprit was housed. The term 'Fish' was used to refer to the ladies from the Volta Hall. So, for instance, when we were going to chase after the ladies, we'd say we were going to fish from the Volta pond).

It was lunch time and as members started trooping in from lectures, they got excited and called for emergency meeting. Meanwhile, a month earlier another lady from the same K block had been caught having romance with one of the errand boys in her room. So that evening, we decided to take the law into our hands, went on proce to Volta Hall to pull the lady out to disgrace her. Unfortunately for us the lady had gotten wind of it and left to an unknown place. But we'd not leave without any action. We cartooned her and plastered her door with condoms. Later we learnt she had rather taken refuge in a friend's room on a different block. The following day in the afternoon we heard she had been rushed to the nearby Legon hospital for attempting suicide by drinking a poisonous substance. We then started receiving condemnation especially when it was reported again late in the evening that her condition had worsened, and she had been airlifted to the major 37 Military Hospital. For the next week or so the *vandals* particularly, me became the target of silent jeers and whisperings. Fortunately, it came out that she had survived. Yet that did not spare us the verbal attacks. Interestingly, the verbal attacks on us were done undertone for fear of incurring our displeasure again. The other Halls, especially Legon Hall, took the advantage and started expressing their support for Volta Hall. They even teamed up and published cartoons of us as animals who should be chased to the forest. Series of unpleasant exchanges followed which made us take decision to break our 'alliance' with Volta Hall ladies.

Why all this long narrative? I want to draw attention to how this couple remembered me still after all these 31 years. It was by my dress/clothing/garments. In Acts 9:3639, when the disciple Lydia died, she was remembered by her sacrifice of dresses/clothing/garments she provided for people. And it is by these garmentssacrifices that brought her back to life. Our sacrifices to humanity go a long way to position us in the full deity of God/Jesus thereby establishing us as an authority in both the kingdoms of life and death. Apart from the literal interpretation of garments representing our sacrifices, it is also an icon of our status/identity/dignity in the society. When the ordinary citizen stops a driver by the roadside, not much attention is paid to him. But when the policeman in police uniform does so, all eyes immediately pop up and the idea of perceived extortion is established. Or what about the Priest who says there is no salvation in wearing the cassock, so he'd prefer putting it in his room and rather goes out in his ordinary shirt and trousers? Disguised identity? Let's be mindful that our sacrifices/services and inherent qualities are pathways that lead us to the world of righteousness.

A Vandal! And So, What?

Don't dare attack a Vandal. Every institution or household would not be happy when you attack one of their lots. Attack one of them and you incur the wrath of all of them. But I have not seen this manifest more uniquely than among the Vandals of Commonwealth Hall of the University of Ghana. I remember somewhere in 1986/87 when a theft by a member of Volta Hall sought to implicate me, the Vandals descended heavily on Volta Hall in my solidarity. Not because I was the culprit but because I was innocent and the lady in question's attitude sought to discredit me. Attack a Vandal and you incur our wrath. But what most people do NOT know is Vandals do NOT tolerate and approve misdeeds by their members; rape, theft, disobedience to norms, indiscipline, etc. Let any Vandal commit any misdeeds and he'd be dealt with drastically than even an outsider.

Christians today have taken the name of God and the canopy of Christ for granted, thereby commuting all sorts of misdeeds. We relish in the name of God/Christ and commit the worst of misdeeds thinking we'd go unpunished. Wives insult and carry out the worst of deeds towards their husbands under the claim "I am a wedded wife in church". Most Christians misbehave at the workplace assuming their bosses dare not reprimand them because "we are the apple of God's eyes". Men of God do all sorts of misdeeds and claim "touch not the Lord's anointed". Our political arena and civil institutions are filled with Christians, yet they are the very people who indulge in worst forms of exploitation of the citizenry. Yes, God says *touch not my anointed, he who touches you touches me*. But the same God says *I'll spew you out of my mouth*.

Do not take the name of God for granted. Yes, Vandals support their lot but will punish them when they misbehave. In a more serious dimension God will deal with those of us who claim to be His yet misbehave. Be careful with your deeds. A Vandal? A Christian? And so, what?

The Nuclear War Between the Mind and Eyes: A Torture for the Head

They say when two elephants fight, the grass and trees suffer. Both the mind and the eyes are located in the head. If they were to engage in a nuclear war against each other, what troubling it would be for the head! What do I mean?

Let me use the story of Joseph as illustration. Joseph enjoyed the comfort of his father's protection, pampering and other special favors over all his brothers (Genesis 37:13). Then all of sudden he lost all and found himself in prison (Genesis 39:120). Even those he once helped, forgot to help him out back (Genesis 40:123). What a torture, if he were to cast his mind back over all the lost blessings as against the challenges that he was seeing now in his life. That's what some of us find ourselves in now. We cast our *mind* back over the privileges that we once enjoyed; the good job we had, the anointing that was upon us, the monies we had in our bank accounts, the numerous foreign trips, the peaceful marriages, etc. But now we behold the challenging situations we find ourselves in now; joblessness, stripped off of anointing, begging for support, insults at our back, being called all sorts of names, rent, bills, etc. We feel like giving up all hopes of coming out. We feel like drinking our heads off. Some may even consider suicide, etc.

But as Joseph trusted in his God and was restored (Genesis 41:146), let us continue to trust Him. The waiting is indeed painful. But let's hang on. When we allow the *mind* to go back to our lost privileges and compare with what our *eyes* see now, we may bring psychological nuclear war upon ourselves.

In qua regione facta sunt nostri, aut non audisti?

In the Greek mythology book *Aeneid* by Virgil, the hero Aeneas, boasting of the heroic achievements of himself and his warriors, made this famous saying **in qua regione facta sunt nostri, aut non audisti?* *(Latin: In which region are our heroic deeds not known on earth and to the gods?). But I'd rather say, where have we not gone to seek solutions to our problems? What haven't we done to come out of our troubles? We have done all that we considered as right channels. We have approached all friends/acquaintances we thought could help us. We have over and over and over again/repeatedly

- fasted,
- offered offerings,
- asked for forgiveness,
- engaged in spiritual warfare,
- stayed and prayed all night heaping judgmental fire upon our enemies,
- carried out directives as recommended by our prophets,
- been soaked with all sorts of anointing oil

- carried all sorts of stickers and tokens on our cars, doorpost, office desks, etc.

    Yet, we haven't received what we expect(ed). Like Job, *"I go to the east, he is not there; to the west, I can't find him* (Job 23:8). So, what do we do now?

- Enough of these frantic efforts. Jesus was offered as a perpetual sacrifice only once for our sake. There's nothing more I'd force myself to do. Let me therefore relax and give all up to God. Let me rather occupy myself with what He deserves best; praise and worship, even in these trial moments (Habakkuk 3:1719), hoping that the words of Daniel may manifest on my behalf, i.e. *"that the living may know that it is the Most High who rules in the affairs of men"* (Daniel 4:17). He makes things beautiful in His own time.

The Tragic Voices of Tragic Heroes

Not long ago here in Ghana, a whole military officer, late Captain Manama, trained and equipped in defence, military skills, and even to kill, was himself lynched and killed by ordinary 'villagers", not in a military campaign but in an ordinary rural community. Irony of situation or irony of profession, one would say.

More than 2000 years ago, somebody who did all sorts of good and even raising the death, claiming sonship of God, had to cry out for common water, on the Cross "I thirst". (John 19:28). Irony of Creation! Where is the God of creation who created water? What a tragedy to hear of these cases! Tragic Voices of Tragic Heroes! Surely, these are complex yet the unbelievable realities of life. For instance,

- Why should the one, who once dished out money to help the needy, now, be going about begging for some small money to buy himself a sachet of drinking water?
- Why should the person who once opened up and accommodated all sorts of friends now be ignored/despised by the very friends he once associated with?

- Why should the once highly anointed Man of God, now be going around and in deplorable situations as if the God he served never exists.
- Why should the once able man/woman who once paid visits to homes to console with households, now be lying helpless alone on the hospital bed?
- Why should the loving parent who used all his/her resources to raise his/her children now left alone struggling to see somebody so that he can send him to buy him/her a sachet of water?
- Why should the once freegiving church member who used to give to support church programs now be the scorn of the very church he dedicated his/her resources to, even be sidelined by the Pastors/Priests/Church Elders of the same church?
- Why at all should that friend of mine, who once helped me, now come and kneel before me and pleading, *"Please, I need just Ghc30 to go on an important trip. Please help me"*?

Tragic Voices of Tragic Heroes indeed!

On the Bus: Temptation from The Devil or SelfInflicted Adventure?

I am right now (12:27pm Ghana time) on the bus from the KNUST Junction (bus terminal) to my village. We are three on the back seat; me on the left near the window, a guy at the right side, and this nicelooking lady in between us. I have been thinking of my mission to the village. A oneman evangelism. Would it be successful or not? Then I sensed the scratching of this pretty lady's legs against mine on the bus. Sensational attraction. But who says it is intentional on her part? It could be that she is just trying to adjust herself well. So why should I think she is trying to get my attention? And the funny part is, instead of me concentrating on my mission, I am getting attracted to her. How? I turned and looked at no other part of hers than her breasts protruding out of her Vshaped brassieres. *Big trouble oooo.*

Why not at any other part but her breasts? You see, troubles come our way, but it is us ourselves who choose to follow and succumb to the troubles. I could have chosen to look at any other part of this lady, but I have chosen to concentrate on her breasts. Imagine if I fall prey to her and find myself in trouble, can she be blamed? No. Troubles/challenges abound but falling victims to them depends on us. The Bible says there is no temptation that befalls us that is not common (1 Corinthians 10:13). The blame game is becoming too much. Let us turn our energies to our shortcomings and see how to move on rather than always blaming others.

On Stage with Kofi Denis, Jutta, Job and Alan Paton this December

I don't remember which theatre productions I had with the likes of Jutta (Dr. AnoffNtow, DirectorGeneral of GBC), and (Prof.) Kofi Dennis. But what I do remember is as then students at the School of Performing Arts, Legon, we all participated in the School's stage performances to relive various messages of the productions in question; tragedy of 'Oedipus', the revolutionary import of the 'Trial of Dedan Kimathi', the morality of the 'Dilemma of A Ghost', the anxiety of 'Waiting for Godot', the satire of the 'Marriage of Anansewaah', etc.

In the biblical book of Job, Job bemoaned the day on which he was born because of the calamities that came his way later in his life. (Job 3:213). I always condemn him. Does Job mean to say that all through his life, until his calamities, he never enjoyed any aspect of blessings in his life? (Job 29:225). Think of the number of children he had, the livestock, labourers, etc. Why then overlook all these and condemn the day he came to this world? It's simple. There are times you don't expect to see/experience certain developments within the context of the period of time.

That is why, today, I too join in the chorus of Job in respect of this month, December:

As a Christian, I bemoan the extent to which unscrupulous 'Men of God' would use the occasion to deceive and exploit the body of the church for their personal glory.

- As an African traditionalist, I bemoan the extent to which the morals and virtues of the ancestors would be condemned and abused.
- As a Social Scientist, I bemoan the extent to which morality would be ignored and humanity abused.
- As a humanitarian, I bemoan the extent to which robbery would be undertaken to rob people of their possessions.
- As a responsible parent, I bemoan the extent to which spouses would abuse their matrimonial beds to the destruction of the welfare of their children.
- And as an unrecognized hero, I bemoan the extent to which the silent voices of unsung heroes in the society would continue to be overlooked.

Help us O Lord, as vileness prowls everywhere in the society. (Psalm 12:8) as we cry with the late Alan Paton of South Africa in crying out, *Cry, Cry the Beloved Country!*

The apostles of Accra Haasto and the Church in Berea

Yesterday I had to travel to Haatso in Accra for a very important meeting. Despite schooling at the University of Ghana in Accra, I had lost my bearings to where exactly Haatso is in Accra. I had to ask my daughter's friend Edwina and my friend Sappiro for location. So, from Kumasi, I got down at Pokuase, took taxi to Kwabenya, then trotro to Haatso. Alighting at the Haatso main station, I asked a guy who said was a resident there for direction to the hotel I was going to." *Oh, not far. Just around the corner after that junction*, he assured me. So why take taxi cab? I walked. But what was to be a 3 minutes' walk took me about 45 minutes merrygoround. Wrong information and direction! Sure, the hotel was few minutes' walk from the station, but the chap rather gave the opposite direction.

    We are told in Acts 17:1011, that the people of Berea critically searched the scriptures to make sure that what the apostles taught them were so. Unfortunately, this is not so with the church body in our times. People are being deceived and led astray by wrong teachings and information. Let's sit up and stop swallowing any message that comes from false 'apostles' and the pulpits.

Moses and Family Planning Methods in Midian

I am not challenging it. I don't ignore it. I don't downplay it. But I try not to get too much disturbed by it. It had been associated with my life before. And I have heard of it before several times. But I was taken aback when I this afternoon overheard a guy explaining to his colleague the reason for of his intention to divorce his wife. What is It? That is, there are certain communities/towns/families which, when you pick a wife from, you end up being a failure in life. He was telling his friend how a certain Man of God had told him he was having problems because agents of evil from his wife's hometown had vowed to make sure any outsider who marries from the town does not prosper. Very worrying assertion indeed.

So as usual I tried to go into the scriptures and digest it in line with similar cases. Moses, running away from the wrath of Pharaoh in Egypt, went to sojourn in the foreign land of Midian. Here, he eventually married a woman, Zipporah, from that land (Exodus 2:15-22). Whatever challenges that Moses might have encountered in his forty years in Midian, he was more of a success than a failure. He was able to give birth to two children in fulfillment with God's decree in the Garden of Eden; to be fruitful and replenish the earth (Genesis 1:28). It was whilst in Midian that God called, commissioned and empowered him to lead Israel out of Egypt. (Exodus 3). In Midian he was knighted with the mantle to be a god to the powerful throne of Pharaoh (Exodus 7:1). And instead of being fought against by the spiritual agents of Midian, he enjoyed the full support of the high priest of Midian who also happened to be his inlaw (Exodus 2:20&21/4:18/18:127).

I am therefore of the view that any true believer and worshipper of God needs not fail wherever he finds himself. To me, experiencing failure just because you marry from a particular family/hometown/tribe holds no water. Not even in marriage alone but in all aspects of our lives. The Bible says anyone born of God overcomes the world. (1 John 5:4) Families, towns, tribes are far lesser than the entire world. And if you overcome the bigger world, how then do you succumb to the lesser family, town, or tribe? It doesn't hold.

The Two Fire Fighters on The Battle Lines of The Samaritans

I have come to admire the stubbornness of the Samaritans who refused Jesus' entry through their village. (Luke 9:5156). This is stubbornness based on frankness not on hypocrisy. Samaritans and Jews at that time did not get on well and these Samaritans were not going to pretend as if they liked Jesus himself a Jew. They had heard of Jesus. His fame had traveled beyond borders (Mark 1:2328/Matthew 9:2326). But they were not ready to compromise. This brings to the scene the issue of being welcomed and/or being accepted. The act of the Samaritan bordered more on acceptance than welcoming. They were not ready to accept Jesus let alone welcome him to pass through their village prompting two of his disciples wanting to call down fire.

Most times we get 'fooled' by the two. The fact that people welcome us does not mean they have accepted us into their midst, to be part and parcel of them. The fact that you are given entry visa into, e.g., Britain/USA/Canada doesn't mean they accept you as one of them. To be accepted, you need to go the extra mile. It has two dimensions. Either you prove yourself worthy of it. Or you yourself become a victim of it. Many a people have suffered from this reality, a reality that is hidden yet leads us into trouble. Why? Because we get carried away by it. Politicians, Men of God, sportsmen, etc. all suffer from it. People in love suffer from it. We get deceived by the face value of people only to realize that deep down in their hearts we are far from their interests. Be careful in your dealings. Make sure people not only sing your praises but also provide the tissue for you to wipe your tears in the days of your calamity.

The Virgin Mother Mary Weeps from Abu Dhabi

As I write this piece from my hidden abode, this Sunday 4th March 2018 morning, 9:36am, a lot of you would be in church already. And for the Catholic, Sunday is one of great significant days with regard to the liturgical services of High Mass, most especially during a Lent season as we are in now. There have been repeated instances of reports about the statue of Mary shedding tears in certain parts of the globe, for instance the one in Tapaon, Vietnam (2017?). Whilst some of other faiths have seen this in negative terms, Catholics have prided themselves in it. Significantly, we have interpreted these reports in terms of (Mary, the Mother of God crying for) the evangelism and conversion of the world. What a noble cause hoping it to be so.

But I beg to twist it a bit. I dare say Mary rather is weeping over the woes of the Catholic Church more than the entire world, a church that apparently holds so much reverence to the commitment of a mother who gave all her life to further the cause of Jesus' mission on earth. Though other faiths and sectors have had their fair share of attacks and condemnations over certain acts, recent exposures of misconduct in the Catholic Church should be of great concern to the Catholic; sexual scandals, exploitation of nuns, financial mismanagement, disrespect of the clergy toward authority, moral decadence, and even spiritual manipulations against each other among the clergy. Please, hold on. Hold on. Don't be angry with me. If I have touched on your emotions, I am sorry. I am not an outsider to the Catholic faith. Despite my evangelical inclinations, I pride myself with a bottomless depth of love for the Catholic faith. And that is why I am joining the 'weeping statue of Mary' to shed tears of exposure not cover up. Instead of covering it up, instead of brushing it aside, instead of seeing it as attack on the church over these scandals, I want to recommend the following;

- Let's be bold to accept that something unacceptable is really happening,
- Let us pray deeply for God (perhaps mother Mary and angelic intervention) to cause a great spiritual renewal in the church.
- Let the Priests who indulge in such shameful acts be bold and resign. They should forget about the 'sweetness' in the priesthood; free education, respect from the laity, free feeding, free accommodation, free cars, etc. and bow out.
- And for you ladies out there, especially the womenfolk groups, St. Theresas, Christian Mothers, etc., stay away from the priests. I know what I am talking about. It bleeds my heart to see my colleagues fall into these crucibles of condemnations.

Sin to Save

After our performance of my script "Save To Save" at the KATH nursing school in Kumasi somewhere in 1984, one of the patrons walked up to me and said that was a great piece but didn't agree with the moral behind it. The script told the story of how a young chap, Gino, in trying to save his parents' marriage, went in for his father's young fiancée who was the cause of the parents' marital breakdown. Many at times people say the end justifies the means. Of course! Jesus had to be killed in other to save us from eternal damnation. But is it always a justifiable cause to resort to the negative to save a situation? Do we have to get our opponents killed in other to win political contests? Do we have to murder and steal to satisfy our needs? Do Men of God have to manipulate the church to believing in the prosperity gospel? Do we have to rape teenagers to satisfy our sexual desires?

This afternoon, on the trotro bus from Effiduase to Kumasi, when we got to Ejisu the driver parked and took on passengers at an authorized point. A police officer came in to 'arrest' the driver. A lady passenger who apparently knew the officer intervened and stopped the arrest. As we drove on, the woman 'boasted' of *'my brother is a police man. Many a times he has helped *offenders* from being arrested. In fact, because of this he has put up a nice storey building from the people he has helped'.*

Interesting but not surprising. We are in a society where the wrong pays more than the right. But should this be the case? Preserve us O Lord from this generation. For the wicked prowl on every side and vileness is exalted everywhere. Psalm 12:8.

Alexander Fu Sheng & The Snake Fist

For those who may not know, Alexander Fu Sheng was a great martial arts film star from Hong Kong (1954‑83). He was a key star in the 70s. The snake fist was/is one of the numerous martial arts styles. Though snakes could be found in trees, their normal movement is on the ground. When Moses, upon God's directive, put his staff on the ground, it turned into a snake. This was the same staff which was to be his tool of wonders to lead the Israelis the Promised Land (Exodus 4:1-4).

God has endowed each of us with specific skills/gifts/potentials, but it is only when we operate them in their specific areas we can actually succeed. In ministry for instance, some of us have been called to be teachers but not prophets, pastors not evangelists. Yet we all try to operate in the prophetic and when we don't function well, we resort to juju or other ungodly means. In politics, the fact that you were once a good Communications Minister doesn't guarantee you to be a President (Did you hear that, Oga?) In business, some of us tend to venture into areas of others and ignore where our potential is. Etc.

Let's take time to carefully identify what our potential is and, most especially, its proper area of operation so as to succeed in life.

The Dead Fowl Fight

The other day, I witnessed a very funny scene at Ejisu. Two grownups were fighting over a fowl knocked down by a car. In the past when we were children, I remember vividly, leftover food would be thrown away the following day. It was thought not good anymore. People would ignore and throw away knocked down sheep, goat, fowls, etc. But today, what do we see? Leftover food can be heated over and over for human consumption. Dead fowls are prepared and put in the fridge for reuse. Man can now turn what was bad into good/acceptable commodity. Why then can't God, the Creator Himself, turn your 'useless' situation for your good? It's just a matter of going before Him with your 'worthless' situations. Pile all to Him, and His microwaves and deep freezers would do the trick.

- All things work for good for those who love and call on Him. (Romans 8:28).
- Rottenness to become sacred (Jeremiah 31:3840).
- Valley of Baca of dead bodies to become springs of living water (Psalm 84:6&7).
- Desert to become fresh greener garden of Eden (Isaiah 51:3).

Not for Me. But for Them

Watching the news bulletin, the other day on the TV, I couldn't help being excited as I pointed out, to my children, my former roommate who had been appointed by the President to head one of the most enviable institutions in the country. Later when I retired to my room, I began to think of my colleagues who are now occupying big positions; some in government, civil service, the security services, etc. I nearly felt left out. Out of near depression, I felt asleep. In my dream, I was sitting on top of a high rock with an old lady with grey hair. Then I saw most of the colleagues who were in those high positions passing by; some with files, executive bags, suitcases, etc. They all appeared busy. The old lady looked at me and saw depression on my face. Then smiling she told me, *"They need your help"*. No not me. I need their support. Then she continued, *"You see, you are depressed because you are not where they are. They have greater responsibilities. But your small support can help them shoulder those responsibilities. Pray for them to shoulder those responsibilities. Your prayers will lend support to God's hands for elevating them"*. I suddenly felt relieved and started smiling. How true. We most often tend to feel depressed, left out, jealous, envious, weakened, to see people in successful positions higher than us. But that is when they need our prayers. When we are left at home and they sit at their offices, we can use our 'idle' time to pray for them. In so doing we thank God for their lives and open our own floodgates of blessings.

When we lift our hearts of praise to God for others, we expand our territories for God's greater blessings to come to us.

When Kumasi Took Over Takoradi

For 22 years I have lived and had almost my entire professional career in Takoradi in the Western region of Ghana. But few weeks ago, I decided and have relocated to my birthplace, Kumasi in the Ashanti region of Ghana. This morning as I sat behind and consumed a ball of banku and okro sauce with seasoned fish, I made one conclusion, that is, indeed a day in Kumasi is far better than 22 years in Takoradi. The psalmist related this experience to God's grace when he said in Psalm 84:10 that "*a day in your courts Oh Lord, is better than a thousand elsewhere*". My breakfast today seems to confirm this.

Reacting to this message above, a reader queried, so did I mean to say that, in all the 22 years I spent in Takoradi, I never experienced any good thing? Just one day food that Kumasi provided, all blessings I received in Takoradi have been forgotten; the peace, shelter, friends and "friends", the call of God and impartation that came upon me there, etc. Just one day banku and okro sauce, all these blessings of Takoradi have vanished. Sad, painful and unfortunate! But that is who we all are.

- Just one challenge and we forget all other blessings God has showered upon us.
- How painful it is for children to forget all the pains and sacrifices parents go through to bring them up, but they end up despising/abandoning these parents when they grow up.
- How unfortunate it is for a father to forget the delicate life of his child but goes ahead and murders him for rituals/money.
- How unfortunate it is that many Men of God have fallen and lost all the many years of unction upon them just because of one act of lust or an avoidable mistake.
- How unfortunate it is that just because of one meal many people have lost their lives through food poisoning.
- How unfortunate it is that a man would forget all the toils and commitment of his spouse and rather goes in for a mistress whilst turning away the spouse.
- How unfortunate it is that just because of earthly power, a politician would go all out to try eliminating his fellow human being.
- How sad it would be that after all the years we spend on this earth, we'd end up losing eternal life in future just because we fail to acknowledge and accept the salvation grace of God through Jesus.
- Remember, it is accountable unto man to die once, and after that judgment.

The Appian Way At SAHUUS

In our days at St. Hubert Seminary (SAHUSS) in Kumasi, despite being fed well from our dining hall, some us still found the extra taste to supplement that. So, in the evening we'd take the (secrete) route behind our classrooms block, by the girls' dorm, and go to the bungalows of the labourers where one of theirs was selling kenkey and okro sauce. We referred to this place as the "Marché noire"(black market) and the route to the place "Appian Way". The Appian Way/road was one of the most important and strategic routes of ancient Roman that led to their conquests. In the book of John, during one of the feasts of the tabernacles, the expectation by the people of Jesus attending was very high for whatever reasons. Even his own family sought to push him to attend in their own way. But Jesus ignored them and went by a secret "apian way". (John 7:228). What an opportunity for Jesus to have seized to market himself as his family suggested.

But he ignored their recommendations.

- We often allowed ourselves to be led by procedures/suggestions/negative status quo, to greatness that are not of God. So, we kill, steal, slander, defraud, manipulate, evil rituals, political murders, cheating, etc.

- Even in Christendom we give in to teachings/doctrines, e.g. prosperity gospel and prophetic releases, which force us to find all means to claim our breakthroughs.

- In the other dimension, which appears frustrating, it is when we/the society expect us to have made it, that we find ourselves in the dark. For instance, people cannot understand why you of all people should be sick, jobless, demoted, or sacked despite being an anointed and committed Man of God.

But as Jesus said on the last day of the feast (John 7:37&38), though your time seems to be running out in its last days, if only you believe in him/God, breakthroughs like fountains of living waters would come to you and through you to others who are also in need.

Qui Se Ressemble S'Assemble: Birds of The Same Feathers Flock Together

I thought I had friends. But as time went by, I started losing them. Even those whom I considered to be of the same feathers: common interests, relatives, Hall associates, class, tastes, same hobbies, civil associations, etc. They are all leaving my flock. I am not avoiding them. Rather they have had their own reasons to fly and fly away from my nest. So, I found/find myself as the lone ranger, moving on across the bridge of life. Then I look around and find something interesting.

- Isn't it interesting that somebody, despite a monthly salary that could feed an entire village, could still have whateversanity of mind, to use his public office and defraud the state and still have followers openly backing him?

- Isn't it amazing that some people can make, what to me is, irresponsible statements publicly and still have high profile personalities supporting them?

- Isn't it intriguing that government can have functionaries openly defending its stance on policies/MOUs/agreements that are against the interest of the citizenry?
- Isn't it funny that we behold what we all know to be insanity among the churchbody, yet some followers go all out to be deceived and fanatically swallow every damned teaching that come out of the pulpit?
- Isn't it astonishing to see people openly defending what is accepted as the unacceptable in the name of human rights?

So, I sit down and ask myself, *"where do you fit in, Joe? Which flock do you fly with?"* None. So where do I go? The Bible says that though we live in this world, our citizenship as believers in Christ is not of this world (Philippians 3:20). If so, and you are a loneranger like me then this is where you need to stand up and live accordingly. Be not conform to the pattern of this world. Make every effort to live every day in the Presence of God. Some associate with party followers, others with school alumni. Some associate with satanic deities and others with occult colleagues. Some associate with their sexual orientation members, others with business interest groups.

What group, what group at all should I focus on now that I find myself on my own? Let me see. Oh yeah. Why not angels of God? True. Yes. That's it. Who are yours?

David! David! David!

Consider the greatness of King David. Israel was not a mere nation. The Individual Israelite was a force to reckon with. Yet David alone valued more than 10,000 of individuals put together (2 Samuel 18:3). Again, he was the 'light of Israel' as a nation. Yet, he didn't trust too much in this status/personality when advised. David could have been killed by the enemy if he had not taken the advice given to him (2 Samuel 21:1517). Many a times we become too much proud and rely on our profile instead of listening to advice. We take things for granted only to turn around and blame others for the troubles that come upon us.

- As a government, we become too much arrogant and take the citizenry for granted. And when we lose power, we blame the other party for vote rigging.

- As Men of God, we feel too much anointed and feed fat on the allegiance of the laity. Then when we are brought to book, we call fire because they should not 'touch my anointed'.

- As spouses we take the love and care of our partners for granted and become arrogant/abusive/disrespectful. And when the partner calls for divorce, we blame family witches for bringing our marriages down, or blame the partner for infidelity.

- As successful businessmen, we make mess of our fortunes. Then when the table turns around, Satan becomes the champion of our fate.

What should we do? We need to be brave and go down on our knees to ask God to teach us wisdom and direct our footsteps instead of 'emptying' His armory to send down fire to consume our perceived enemies. (Luke 9:54).

Where Is Bepo Yaw, The Smoking Mountain?

Bepo Yaw is a rocky mountain at my hometown, KunsuWioso in the Ahafo Ano South in the Ashanti region, Ghana. The town lies beneath it. It sorts of towers and overshadows the town. A natural banner, I'd say. What does the Bible say? *"In the last days, the mountain of the Lord's temple shall be established as the chief mountain. And people will say, let us go to the mountain of the Lord"*. (Isaiah 2:24). Banners, billboards, posters, etc. I don't have problem with the erection of and installing sign posts and occasional banners to announce a program. I mean Christian activities/programs. But I find it absurd and outoforder to see Men of God spending huge sums of monies in giving directions to their/churches. Huge billboards, sign posts, posters, etc. Aren't we raising ourselves, instead of God? Almost every day when you turn the TV on or tune in to the radio, you find 'Men of God', fervently giving directions as to where they can be found and how listeners/viewers should follow up on them. They 'preach' for few minutes ministers and the rest is directions or phone numbers.

Yet our Lord Jesus ironically sought to hide Himself from being publicized, e.g. John 7:1012. Why don't we allow our good deeds speak for us, if indeed we believe we are truly called by God and we too are committed to this call without any selfish interest?

The most absurd thing is that these publicity gimmicks are paid from 'fleecing' the believers, believers who are manipulated to believe in the anointing of the Man of God instead of being exposed to the true teachings of the Word of God. There are numerous poor people whom the cost of these publicities could help yet we ignore them and rather 'misuse' the money for our selfish goals. Misplaced and abuse of resources. So just because the people are prepared to sow seed to support us means we should we abuse their trust in us? Don't let's take the faith of the people for granted. A time will come, and it's coming, when the Hand of God will pull us down if we continue to raise ourselves above the humility of His sacredness.

Upon the Wings of Lucky Dube

Dear Lord Jesus, adapting and modifying the lyrics of Lucky Dube's song "Remember Me", I today make the following urgent prayer.

Daddy wherever you are, remember me.
In whatever you do, I love you.
You left this world many years ago,
Promised to come back for us.
Many years have gone by but still no sign of you, O Lord,
Many have died of heartbreaking challenges.
Perhaps our sins have kept you away from us,
But you are the only solution we have.
So, Lord, wherever you are, help us out.
In whatever our sins, we love you.
So, Lord, wherever you are, remember us,
And provide us with our needs.
Wondering up and down, the streets of challenges,
With no place to go for solace.
We have tried to find answers on our own,
But still no sign of solutions.
So, Lord, wherever you are, remember us.
And in whatever our sins, we look up to you. Amen.

Our City. Who Is to Prophesy?

Jephthah entered into a covenant of success that harbored on his daughter's fate. He covenanted with God that if God would give him success in a battle he was going to, he'd offer up as an offering whatever comes out of his doors to meet him. He won. His daughter came out first. The innocent girl, who didn't know of this secret covenant and was about to begin full life, had to die (Judges 11:3139). Today, I am focusing on our political leaders and Heads of our institutions. Some of our leaders have engaged in secret deals for their own selfish interest to the detriment of the society. In our innocent minds, we cherish them. Yet, their schemes have put the life of our children at stake. In Ezekiel 11:2, God lamented over the leaders who were plotting iniquity in the city (Ezekiel 11:2). Secret deals of loot and share. Secret deals of contract commissions. Secret deals of budget inflations. Secret deals of spiritual covenants. They speak against hardships, yet they are the very few who plan to the woes of the majority. And as God asked Ezekiel to speak/prophesy against it (Ezekiel 11:4), it is up to our religious leaders to now come out boldly. The woes of this country and the continent are NOT only spiritual. It is conscious sitdowncalculatedschemes by some of our leaders. Of course, the spiritual covenants cannot be ignored. It is still up to us to handle that instead of tackling only the witches/demons in people's families. "Son of Man, speak out. Prophesy against them". (Ezekiel 11:4).

Abraham's Quota: Is the Situation All That Bad? What about the 7000 Diplomats?

- There was a time, precisely February 2007, when all the entire UNDP staff in Nigeria went on a retreat to the northern sector of Kaduna. I was then their UNV Program Officer. In the course of the trip, I happened to engage in a chat with one of the elderly members of staff, Mr. Anthony Dioka. He told me that God had positioned His agents at strategic locations on earth to fulfill His mission. And that these people don't even know themselves. In the book of Genesis, we find Abraham defending the destruction of Sodom and Gomorrah with ten righteous people out of the entire population in that territory. Unfortunately, this quota could not be met (Genesis 18:32&33). Just few righteous people needed to save a catastrophe. I am one of people who 'complain and criticize' the perceived abuse by Men of God and people in strategic positions. Constantly bashing at them like the condemning voices of Ezekiel, Jeremiah, and Amos.

But I am also asking myself, is the station all that bad? Don't we have at least ten genuine Men of God/believers who can be trusted to fulfill God's purpose on this earth and in our lives? I don't think the situation is that bad. What I think is needed is for us to stop complaining beyond measure and see how we too can help address the situation. Who knows, you might be one of the ten righteous people needed to save the situation.

- ***The 7000 Diplomats***

I was once in charge of a refugee project which provided for about 7,000 refugees in one camp only. They received special attention as far as the UNHCR mandate was/is concerned. Special people with special focus. When the prophet Elijah once complained about the vices and woes in the society, God told him He had hidden 7,000 genuine prophets who didn't fall for the vices, bowing to Baal, in the society. (1 Kings 19:18). Elijah was taken up believed to be in the presence of God monitoring 7,000 genuine diplomats/ambassadors of God. The population in individual countries like Ghana, Nigeria, the African continent, Europe, the Caribbean, USA, is more than 7,000. Are you one of the 7,000 that God would be proud of? Are you one of the 7,000 politicians who are not looting the State? Are you one of the 7,000 Christians not condoning vices? Are you one of the 7,000 Men of God not exploiting and misusing the Name of God/Christ? Are you one of the 7,000 civil servants not stealing from the national purse? Are you one of the 7,000 security agencies that do not secretly support crime in the society? Are you one of the 7,000 youth whose lifestyle is not against the moral values of the society? Can God point you out to Elijah and say, 'Joe Adus is one of the 7,000 people I talked about'?

Oh Lazarus!
Oh Ohenenana Angela.

Yesterday, I attended the burial rites of the late Ohenenana Angela Pokuaa Kufuor at Ayigya in Kumasi. She was the younger sister of my Sixth Form School mate, Carol Kufuor. For some personal reasons, I had no excuse to absent myself. I attended with other two of our colleagues, (Rev.) Steven Owusu Afreh and Mrs. Victoria Duah. The deceased also had family ties with Ex President Kufuor and the Asante royal stool. So, you could imagine how big the event was. What has Christ got to do with this? As I sat quietly and was observing all the proceedings, my mind went to the biblical event of Jesus raising Lazarus from death in John 11. I began to discourse in my mind the unique deity of Jesus. What kind of deity did Jesus possess and could still be functional in our lives? Of course, it's not only the Christian bible that attests to His deity. Other faiths do so as well.

- When Lazarus died, was he buried straightaway without embalmment? If so, then this accounts for the already decaying nature of the corpse when Jesus arrived at the scene, as Martha said in John 11 verse 39. And so, if at this stage, Jesus through some divine authority brought him back to life, then surely Jesus carried the secret key to death and life. (Revelation 1:18/John 11:2527). What a unique deity!

- And if Lazarus was preserved for some time through some sort of embalmment before burial then it wasn't a thorough embalmment. This also justifies the decomposing state. But the interesting fact here is that, even if not thorough embalmment, at least some inner parts of the corpse would have been taken out or tampered with before burial. How could a corpse which has lost some inner parts come back to life? Yet it happened. Again, Jesus scoring unique marks here. Surely, Jesus was more than what the human nature could justify and understand. No wonder the Bible says he carried the full deity of God Himself (Colossians 1:19&20). And no wonder his name still continues to influence humanity.

May the souls of the faithful departed rest in Peace!

The Possibility of the Impossibility

A young man walked to me the other day and sadly complained,

"*Man of God, I hear most times about God visiting Sarah and Abraham with a child in their old age. But theirs was just *one problem*, barrenness. Mine is different. I keep messing up with the blessings that come my way. I rise and fall. Not once but several times*".

He was very much depressed. I was confused myself. Not knowing how to respond, I stared at him quietly for some time. Then I found something that soothed him, something I am sure it is true.

Yes, Sarah was said to be barren. But what sort of barrenness? I am of the view that she did conceive several times in her prime, but the pregnancy kept getting spoiled/destroyed always due to ectopic or some gynecological problem. No wonder she never thought she could ever have a child (Genesis 21:6 & 7). You see, sometimes we assume we have the worse of problems. We give up when our challenges keep on repeating. The young man had similar problems. The same way Sarah might have had repeated pregnancy disorders. But that is when the possibility of the impossibility comes in based on our (stupid) faith in God. Is there anything too hard for the Lord? (Genesis 18:13&14).

The Dark Colored Blood or the Yellowish Cooking Oil?

Whether you support its celebration or not, the fact is, come December 24January 1st, majority of the world would indulge in Christmas festivities. But what baffles me is the extent to which we give too much credence to socalled satanic orchestrations during such a period. Advertised billboards, conferences, fasting and prayer sessions, prophetic convocations, etc. All targeting at Satanic operations. The other day, I heard a prophet telling somebody that witches in his family needed 1000 barrels of human blood during the forthcoming Christmas season, and that he and his children were earmarked as part of those who were going to be killed to produce the 1000 barrels of blood. Excuse me!

In as much as satanic agents exist, I think we most often create unnecessary scenarios. We create too much unnecessary fear and panic. In Nahum 1:15, God assures us of the celebrations of our festivals without any attack by the wicked in any way. All we need is to have good personal relationship with Him. Let's stop creating platform for the devil to operate from. I can foresee a situation where people would be deceived to 'sow seeds' (huge sums of monies especially) all in the name of blocking Satan from spilling their blood. I dare to differ. God is never prepared to allow us turned into sheep, fowls, goats, for witches/wizard to be fed on. No human blood for cooking oil.

Saving the Perishing.

Let's save the perishing not from satanic orchestrations but from wrong indoctrination, false teachings and manipulating revelations. Christmas is approaching and the wolves in sheep skins would do their tricks to bleed the sheep. Join my rural outreach visits/campaigns. Where do you want to participate/support?

- A speaker.
- Provision of PA system.
- Cash for transportation, chairs, canopies, refreshment, protocols with community leaders?

It's for selected communities. Let me know where you fit in.

Not Extra Time Yet

In the finals of a football match at which a winner should be declared by all means, when the 90 minutes end and no winner emerges, extra time of 30 minutes is played out to determine the winner.

At the beginning of this year, we made resolutions and aspired to achieve individual goals by the end of the year: better relationship with God, extend our ministries, get jobs, get married, improved business, come out of our sicknesses, acquire/build houses, etc. 11 months have passed, and we have just entered the 12th month today. But as at now, either all or some of us have not achieved what we earmarked for at the beginning of the year. So, do we say, we have scored 11 wasted months?

Let us put this in divine dimensions. God established 12 tribes of Israel from the lineage of Abraham through Jacob (Genesis 46); 12 stones were set up by Joshua to establish the truthfulness of God (Joshua 4:1924); Jesus chose 12 out of the lot to be his apostles (Luke 6:1216); the revealed New Jerusalem would have 12 gates with 12 angels and the names of new breed of the 12 tribes of Israel. (Revelations 21:1012).

(In fact, God's divinity is entrenched in a12 hierarchical realm not 7 as it is generally claimed. I'll explain this someday).

So, for not achieving our set goals, does it mean we have failed? Has God failed us? No. No extra time yet. When Judas felt out of the 12 apostleship, his vacuum was filled (Acts 1:1526). Perhaps something ought to be taken out of our lives. At the same time something ought to be provided. Negative out, positive in. God is still God and the Great Providence at all times in every time. Remember, the time between Abraham raising the knife and striking his son Isaac dead was less than one minute. Yet God intervened within that short time and provided a ram for the sacrifice. Jehovah Jireh indeed. We still have a full month of thirtyone days to go before the end of the month. It is never too late for your aspirations to come through. Nothing is impossible for God.

Exercise:

Let's try this. Choose a day, or 12 days if you can, during this month. Fast for 12 hours and pray God to remove that negative situation in your live: sicknesses, sin, joblessness, financial crisis, addiction, etc. And ask Him to provide that which you need. No extra time yet.

The Father's Mantle

Absalom was a legitimate son of David, loved, respected and treated royally by everyone because of his status as the King's son. But growing seed of pride, success, selfesteem made him turn against his father (2 Samuel 15). He died a miserable death despite his father's prayers to save him (2 Samuel 18: 117). Solomon was sort of the 'bastard' child but eventually became the King.

- Children should know that no matter how educated, successful, 'wiser, they become, they still need to live under the divine covering of their parents. That is "the father's mantle".

- Employees should know that no matter how experienced they become, they owe much to the employer despite shortcomings on the part of the employer/company.

- Associate Pastors should know that no matter how great their anointing, they owe much to their Senior Pastors/ likewise Catholic priests owe much to their Bishop or Archbishop.

- Wives and husbands should equally acknowledge the sacrifices of their partners instead of insulting, cursing and even maltreating each other.

You cannot get away from the covering of the Father's Mantle.

Neutralizing Moses' Weapon of Mass Destruction

In an attempt to avoid God's purpose for his life to lead Israel out of Egypt, Moses had a long argument with God (Exodus 3&4). To prove His determination, God caused Moses' rod/walking stick to turn into a snake and Moses had to flee from it (Exodus 4:3). Remember, this is the same rod Moses had been using all the (40 years) in Midian before the Lord called him. But this time he had to flee from it.

    Life can turn against you at any time. As a Man of God, no matter how powerful you are, you can go dry and fall. In the same way, the once richest guy can find himself begging for support from friends. Despite all his football skills, (my boy) Christiano Ronaldo can miss a penalty. The most astonishing thing about this phenomenon is that in most cases, it is the least expected that turn against us. It is when we don't expect it that we fall down. It is those we least suspect who turn against us. It is when we find ourselves enjoying life that we lose our jobs. When that happens, what do we do? Instead of staying calm and wait for God to restore the situation (Exodus 4:4), we run away. To where? To seek support from where we shouldn't go to. We get discouraged, panic, frustrated, etc. We resort to occult, ritual murders, political manipulations, robbery, deceit, fraud, prostitution, etc. But if we remain calm and wait on the Lord with trust, He will surely turn the tables round in our favor once again (Isaiah: 14:1&2). Remember John Sammis 1887 classical hymn? Trust and Obey!

Takoradi Show Boys and The Chariots of Pharaoh

Are you sure you know Takoradi, the capital of the Western region of Ghana?

The ladies, drinks, the fun, the octopus khebabs, and the beach parties! Anyway, that is not my point of reference today. It is about another area of life.

About 19 years ago, I was combining my secular job with my part time voluntary ministry fellowship sessions like I am doing now. That was in Takoradi. There was this Man of God who became a friend and we used to share ideas. At a point in time, he began to encounter some difficulties. Very disturbing ones. I remember him telling that if he was really convinced it was God who had called him, then he should stay on. There is this saying that nothing works in Takoradi, so you even see most Men of God abandoning the area to set up their ministries in other locations like Accra, Kumasi, Tema and overseas. Today, this Man of God is one most disciplined and powerful genuine but lowprofiled Prophet I have known, still in Takoradi. And I really respect him for that. An example of somebody who believed he owed his life to God and not to any other source.

From the Bible, we learn that from his toddler stages up to age 40, Moses enjoyed great life in the bosom of Pharaoh's kingship;

palace food, spiritual and physical protection, best chariots more splendid than modern day Concord/jets, beautiful women to behold, etc. Then things turned round badly. To make his case serious, he committed the most serious of wrongs; killed a human being, God's own representative. So, from palace life, he now found himself serving as a mere slave shepherd in Midian, cast away from the opportunities that came his way (Exodus 2: 1122).

But because Moses was God's call, things worked out for him even at age 80 plus.

I often hear people talk of lost glories. It is as if we have lost it all especially if you consider that time is running out on you, especially for those of us aged 50+. Yes, we once enjoyed life, had the best opportunities, great ministry life, massive following, etc. but now find ourselves out somewhere in the dark with no job, ministry fall out, sick, begging for bread, rent problems, imprisoned, asked to proceed on leave, lost out political glories, etc. But if all that we once enjoyed was from God, then surely the better than the best is coming up as it worked for Moses and my Man of God from Takoradi. This time round Moses became a god to Pharaoh (Exodus 7:1) He who once killed a human being had angels protecting his corpse from Satan (Jude 9). He became a slaveshepherd in Midian (Exodus 3:1) not knowing that he was representing Jesus the Good Shepherd, who was to come thousands of years later. If truly you are sure that what is yours or what came your way was by God's own means, then keep on looking up to God. Join me relax in the Lord as one would relax at the Takoradi beach resort.

Sitting Under the Ladder with Jacob

Imagine you sitting in the desert of Bethel with Jacob. Then you see all those angels of God coming up and down to you on the ladder. (Genesis 28:12). Will you run away, or stay on, or offer them something, or demand something from them? Think over these options. Well let me come to my message for today by revealing to you one deep revelation of that story. The descent and ascent of the angels means, in life, we come across two categories of people. Those going up/progressing and those coming down, i.e. falling or better still ailing in life due one reason or the other. Life is ups and downs. Wherever you are, you become a central figure in people's lives.

- So, when you see people going up/in higher positions/status than you, do you uphold them or pull them down? We have people whose interest is to assign negative causes to others who have made it to the top. Are you like that?

- On the opposite side, when you see people falling/failing in life, do you support them to be on their feet or even come to your level? Think of how you can be of a support to both the one higher than, and the ones lower than where you are.

The Cry of the Toddler or the Emptiness of the Vitro?

There was once a man who was going through very difficult times. But despite all this he would not allow anything come between him and his family especially his young child whom he'd play with. The child would make sounds and the man would laugh with him though he didn't make any words out of the sounds. Then one day, not being able to endure his hardships any longer, with a heavy heart he decided secretly to leave the family to go somewhere. That morning, as he sneaked out, the child made his usual sounds. Sadness filled the father's heart, he came back to the child and played with him as usual. Unknown to him, his landlord had been watching him every day. That very instant the landlord walked to the man and said *"I have been watching you all this while. If you can be such responsible towards what God has given to you, you can be more responsible for what man would entrust to you. I today employ you to manage my businesses and all other assets."*. The magic of responsibility!

There are many people out there spending millions of cedis/naira/dollars/Euros/pounds to get just one child from vitro fertilization. How thankful have you been to God for the one He has given you despite your challenges?

- There are children going wayward because parents have refused to be responsible.
- There are children sleeping on the streets because their parents have been ejected.
- There are children dying in the hospitals because somebody has embezzled State funds.
- There are children dying of hunger because somebody wants to show his wealth in public for public recognition, even in the church, instead of helping the poor family.
- There are children crying every day because their mothers have been abused violently.

The child in hand is worth more than the emptiness of the glass tube. Help in any way and whenever you can.

Dedicated to the memory of the late Ghanaian teenage music icon, Ebony Reigns, whose spirit now flies to the eternal realms of God.

Eliphaz Said It All

The torture and pain of the challenges that come our way lie in the fact that they come in the very way and time we least expect. Eliphaz, Job's friend, said it all in Job 4:4 & 5;

Your words have comforted many, ….

Your words have upheld him who was stumbling, and you have made firm feeble knees.

But now it has come to you, you are impatient; it touches you, and you are dismayed.

It is easy to tell the one who had lost a dear one to take it easy. But when it comes to you, it is a different matter. How could Jesus be denied by the one (Peter) to whom He entrusted the key of His church! How could you who once served your church with the greatest of commitment as a Minister be, slandered by the very church you loved! How could you who once supported the needy and helped the poor be the one now going around begging for alms! How could you who once opened your doors to strangers, accommodated the shelterless now face ejection! How could you, who once carried the sick on your shoulders, now be looking for someone to take hold of your hands and lead you to the restroom! How could you who gave all your love to your husband now be the victim of unfaithfulness and despise!

But such is the tragedy of life we have to endure. The only way out is to side with Job in saying *I know my Redeemer liveth (Job 19:25)*

Tempus Fugit
(Latin: Time Flies)

And on the ninth hour Jesus cried with a loud voice...and died. (Mark 15:3438)

- Where are you right now?
- What time is it?
- What are you doing right now?
- Reading this book? Where precisely are you?
- Is the place you are right now in line with your vision in life?
- Before reading this book and after you have put it down, what will you do?
- Will that be in line with God's purpose for your life?

Reflect on these questions and decide about your life and its future.

The Wings of Togbe Beyond the Walls of the Vandal City

Yesterday was observed as a holiday in Ghana marking the birthday of our late first President Kwame Nkrumah. Sitting before the TV screen and listening to his uniqueness, vision, projects, policies for not only Ghana but the entire Africa continent, I asked myself *'so where is he now?* Is it true there's a world after this life? Then in the evening I learnt from our Vandals platform that one of our colleagues, Togbe Sedem Klubi has passed on. I was 'knocked down' and shed tears. I am sure some of our colleagues would be wondering why this piece about Togbe in the sense that they did not see too much of closeness between him and me apart from the fact we were all members of Commonwealth Hall, the Vandal City as we sometimes call it. But I tell you, Togbe was very close to me. He was my, I think, two years my senior. My affiliation with Commonwealth Hall, was characterized by boozing and dancing, fun, idolizing of our ideals of Vandalism apart from the normal academic work. During the various Halls Week celebrations of the various Halls of residence at the University, you'd find me publicly dancing sometimes drunk. And Togbe would be there dancing with me, not as drunk as me though. Even though after we graduated and left, we didn't maintain that constant correspondence, we still had in depth interactions the few times we got in contact. I remember, he was once so much concerned about me (jobless) that he wanted to recommend me for a job with the NADMO (National Disaster Management Organization). Fortunately, I got myself an international assignment with a foreignbased NGO so the NADMO move was aborted. Again, not long ago, he was instrumental in reconnecting me to a former lady friend of ours.

Then all of sudden last night I heard of Togbe's death. His spirit and soul have now flown out beyond the Walls of the Vandal City. As a Christian and Man of God, I am sure some of you would find it intriguing for me to ask,

So where is Togbe Now?
Is there really a world out there where Togbe has gone to now?
And is he really there?

The Milkmaid Girl and The Diploma's Daughter

Love? I didn't know anything about love. What was it? Yet something pulled me to her. 6th Form at the allgirls school in Kumasi. Name withheld for integrity reason. We were tuned to each not because she was fair, the obroni kind. And not because I was handsome. Yet some chemistry was taking place within me. We got on well. My younger sister liked her. At times I had to wait for her to be present at Class before me getting focused. I remember introducing her to my colleagues even to my guardians. We sneaked in to moving around in town sometimes. Koo darkie (charcoal blackie) myself and fairyoghurt skin girl. Elements of attraction. Later on, at the University campus, the relationship continued. Mishap happened, and we broke up.

There was also this other lady who later came on the scene. She was my course mate. I really loved her. She was the disciplined and more focused type. Her father was a career diplomat. To me she was from the upper class. So, I couldn't confess my love. I kept it within me. My affection for both at the different points in my life, was it love? What is love? We never thought of sex. Not because of any material gains. Was I the ignorant or the weak type?

Now love has been associated with sex and is play of materialism. I have been thinking of this many times. The Bible talks in John 3:16 of God loving us so much so that He demonstrated this by sacrificing Jesus for us. If love were to be lowered to sex, how many women did God sleep with to show this love? God's love goes beyond mortal emotions even as I cherished my relationship with that fair girl, the milkmaid girl, the Tess of d'Urbervilles kind. Mortal affections have limitations and bound to collapse. But the love of God for us goes beyond our human emotions and expectations.

I pray that you experience this incomprehensible love of God with all the inner joys it entails.

Nakupenda malaika. (I love you my angel/darling).

The Sailing Ships of Don Diego d'Azambujas and Co

For some reasons, those of us from this part of the world, I mean Africans and those of African descent, have had cause to accept Christianity and even the entire Bible with pinch of salt. This is because those who brought down the book (Bible) down to us, from their sailing ships, the likes of Don Diego d'Azambuja of Portugal, have themselves given us cause to 'accuse' them of using the Bible to dehumanize us. They have been accused of the manipulation of our cultural and moral values. Here, one can mention the Slave Trade and colonization/partition of Africa as some of the most infamous evidences.

So instead of isolating the perceived manipulation of our values through the Bible by them, we tend to condemn them together with the Bible/ Christianity. But if those missionaries and their mother nations used the Bible/Christianity to abuse us, does that make the Bible a bad tool? I don't think so. If a neighbor uses my cutlass to clean shit instead of using it to cut bread, does it mean the cutlass is bad? No! The early missionaries and their imperial leaders might have had hidden agenda and manipulated us through the Bible, but that does not eliminate the truthfulness and power of the word of God and Christianity for that matter. In condemning their abuse of our values, let's be careful we don't dump the essential value of the Bible in the life of humanity, of which we are all part. We may condemn the Christopher Columbuses, the Francis Drakes, the Thomas Bakers, the Don Diego d'Azambujas, the David Livingstons, etc. but we cannot ignore the value of the Bible. Sure, we too have our own traditional rich and priceless norms and teachings, but the Bible adds more value to us when properly digested.

Let them be condemned for their apparently abuse of the Bible. But let us refine our lives through that same Bible. It is us not them. Note what Psalm 119:105 says *"Your word is a lamp unto my feet"*

Embarrassment in The Lord?

"Joe, don't be embarrassed. If I may ask, if you feel so much passionate about God, why do such people go begging?

This is what somebody put to me following my post on the 35 days dry fasting the other day. My brother, I know where your question is coming from. And why you are telling me not to be embarrassed by your question, I am not.

But that's part of the complex nature of the world. It is a world of limitations and imperfection. And so long as we live in it, we'd experience limitations. Despite the vastness of the sea, fishermen and sailors still get thirsty at sea. Despite the abundance of air, patients still need and are given oxygen scientifically at the hospital to survive. Despite all his anointing, the prophet Elisha died of sickness (2 Kings 13:14&20). Despite all his wealth and pomp, David at one time had to beg and be insulted by Nabal (1 Samuel 25:1‐11). Despite his sonship to God, the Savior Jesus died on the Cross thirsting for water. (John 19:28). Even despite His all mightiness, God had to contend with Pharaoh in ten major plagues before leading the Hebrews out. (Exodus 11:1‐12:36). God is not measured in human terms. Don't ever allow anybody value God in your terms: your anointing, wealth, status, prayer life, success and failures. (That's why it is very dangerous for Men of God to be carried away by the praise of people over their anointing/exploits). It is you only who can determine the value of God in your life. And this is done in the purity of your faith in heart. So, my brother, if after 35 days fasting some of us are in need, that's not a big deal. I still see the value of God in my life. Be my guest in experiencing God in the heart.

Good Friends We Had, Good Friends We Have Lost

Where is Finbar? Augustine, Joe, Amakye, Janet, Koo Bare, Oga Sako, Papa Yaw, Claire, Clare, Augustine, Jeannette, Jennease, Mike Arthur, Ama Tawiah, Kesson, Mercy Najua, Fr. Dorr CSSp, etc.? These people were once my daily companions at one point in time. Some friends and some relatives. But today, I am without them. Some are already dead. And even those alive among the lot, I still haven't been able to contact them despite advanced technology. So here I am but not with them. But Jesus, and for that matter God, is here and will always be even in eternity. So why don't stick to Him? I know He is always be there for and with me. Matthew 28:20

Joe Adus kidnapped

"*Reports from the security agencies have confirmed that Joe Adusei, once a notorious Vandal of the Commonwealth Hall, University of Ghana, now a Man of God, Joe Adusei, aka Vandal Ninja, Osofo Ninja, Willy Joe, Joe Amit, has been kidnapped around 9pm last night. Family sources say three unknown men entered his house and kidnapped him. No reasons are given yet*".

Immediately after this news broadcast, you would see people expressing their sympathy, some calling home to express their concern and support. Then after one or two days, there comes further news update that the kidnappers are demanding a ransom price of US$ 50,000 (Fifty thousand US dollars.) What would happen? The calls stop. Socalled friends/associates back off. Some even refuse to respond to phone calls. Hmmm.

This morning, a sister on one of other platforms posted the question that if a ransom of $1000,000 (one million dollars) were put on your head, how many of your associates would stand with you. A very thoughtprovoking question. She's talking of $1,000,000. You even bring it down to just Ghc500 equivalent of $114.41/£87.03. How many would come to your aid? Some would block your line, and some would not even pick the calls whilst some would simply respond *"plz I am very busy"*. As for insulting you in your absence, don't mention it. Yet Christ offered himself as a ransom for us free (I Timothy 2:6/John 3:16). So, who is the true friend then?

Tunes in the Grave: Kelvin Kuofi

Apart from few of us in the NGO field at Takoradi, I don't think people knew we were very close. Not even his family and other friends. When I set up the Centre for AIDS Information Network (CAIN) in late 90s, he was one of the only three staff who played active role in establishing an antiHIV/AIDS status quo in the advocacy struggle nationally and internationally. Anytime I traveled abroad he was there to hold the fort. Very hardworking, disciplined and reliable. Even after the folding up of CAIN, and we got engaged in separate jobs, we still maintained the bond of brotherhood. Recently, we again came together to restructure CAIN into the Network for Cultural Orientation and Development Affairs (NECODA) which was inaugurated last year. We were then in the process of still marketing this Network. Few months ago, I relocated to Kumasi whilst he remained in Takoradi still helping me to get this initiative going. Then about three weeks ago, I received a WhatsApp message from a pastor friend asking me if it was true that Kelvin was dead. No. Could it be one of these social media pranks? That was my response. Because I had spoken with him four days before. I was therefore shocked when a close friend confirmed his death. How come?

He was 'healthy' and never showed any sign of suffering from any ailment. I understand he collapsed and was pronounced dead upon arrival at the hospital. Hmmm.

I understand Kelvin was going through some emotional challenges. I can't mention the details here. For me, my pain is that he is gone. I have been crying once a while since I heard of his death. My family too is shocked and saddened. Next week Saturday, he'd be buried. Should I attend or not the funeral? Just to see his corpse and other friends? I don't even know his family. If I go, to whom would that help? Man, indeed, is like the flower. It flourishes in the morning but by sunset he is no more. Kelvin is gone like all other mortals. But there's somebody who remains forever. Even in death, He was alive. And through resurrection, He is, Jesus, the Alpha and Omega. There's is nothing more important than keeping my relationship with Him stronger and in holiness then.

Meanwhile Kelvin, may you continue to be useful even in death, as the termites feed on your corpse when you are buried.

Chorus of the Aged

The other day, I was to travel to Bibiani and the Wassa areas to collect some important data and return. But before then I had to minister and lead prayer sessions in the morning at the Our Lady of Apostles Catholic Church at Gyinyase, Kumasi. I must admit, I wasn't in good spirits at all. And when I entered the church, I saw the usual few oldaged people and some kids. Not the vibrant youth who would need such meetings for their assumed breakthrough. Not a full house for you to feel *'yea God is really using me.'* But what struck me about them was the feel of their total joy in the Lord. As I went on to minister, I could sense the uplifting of their hearts to God. I'd say I was 'anointed' by them instead of me touching them. These are people who have passed their needs for cars, fabulous clothing, prosperous spouses, complex houses, etc. Yet they have found time to come before the throne of God to express their ownership and joy in Him. Amazing.

And this is the message; let's us seek Him/God now that we have the time/opportunity. For a time is coming, and it will surely come, i.e. our old age, when we'd be left alone on our own. In those times, it may be too late to seek Him.

President Nana Addo and Herod's Gift of John the Baptist's Head

Prez Nana Addo of Ghana is proposing a legislative process to officially set August 4th as "Founders Day" in honor of those who led the process of Ghana's Independence and September 21st, the birthday of our first president, as "Kwame Nkrumah Memorial Day".

Herod, according to Matthew 14:611, had John the Baptist beheaded and his head given as a special birthday gift to his illegitimate stepdaughter. As I moved around town today, I could count not less than 21 billboards and posters in favor of some Men of God/Pastors/Prophets, etc. announcing the

- "Honoring Our Father Service",
- "Daddy's Day Celebrations",
- "We Love Our Father Thanksgiving Day",
- " 3 Days Papa's Appreciation Day", etc.

Back home this evening I am asking myself "*Joe, how many posters and billboards are announcing and honoring tomorrow September 19th as your birthday?* Nothing of that sort. And who, apart from my family, am I even sure would remember to wish me a 'Happy Birthday" tomorrow let alone buy me a car/motorbike or even a Bible?

You out there might not have pasted posters or set up billboards for me, I do appreciate you for being part of my life even as I cross another milestone few hours to come tomorrow September 19th: relatives, school mates, course mates, friends, workplace staff, exfiancées, church members, copastors, students, landlords/ladies, cotenants, creditors and debtors, donors, lecturers, etc. Therefore, in a positive vein of Herod's special gift, who gave out a special gift on his birthday, let me appreciate you all for being part of my life in various ways by saying;

- *May the Lord bless you and keep you: May the Lord make his face shine upon you and be gracious on you: May the Lord lift his countenance upon you and give you peace. (Numbers 6:2426) in the NAME of the Father, of the Son and of the Holy Spirit.*

Protocol Officers

As you come to the end of this book, join me shake of some pressure and have fun. Let us assume we are God's Protocol Officers. Let us try then to draw a possible daily routine for Jesus with some assumptions and possible facts.

- That Jesus usually spent all night or dawn in prayers. This means His day time ministry would start around 6am. (Mark 1:35)

- That by the time He started at age 30, He could be staying with His parents or had His own residential facility (John 1:3739).

- That though now a grown up and practicing on His own, it's possible He still went occasionally to help in the family's carpentry work (Matthew 13:35).

- That though He usually traveled abroad with His disciples, He did come to the family house often (John 7:19).

So, let's try and draw his daily activities:

- 6am... Keep fit exercise.
- 6.45am... Toilet and bath.
- 7.15am... Torah and Scriptures reading.
- 8am... Breakfast

- 8.45am... Household chores.
- 9.15am... Daily discourse with His working team, the apostles.
- 10am... Field exercise/Missions.
- 3pm... Visit to the synagogue/ Temple for afternoon prayers.
- 4pm... Home visitations/Games/Playing cards/Work at the carpentry shop
- 6pm... Evening bath.
- 6.30pm... Dinner.
- 7.30pm....Evening prayers with disciples/family.
- 8. 30pm..Retreat to bed.

What do you think?

{A} EXULTATION OF FAITH FOR BLESSINGS/ TEACHING

1. The reason why you are here today is that God has designed for you and would also use that to bless others. For this, He has long time determined not to let anyone or anything destroyed you. Moreover, He has made you untouchable by the power of His grace through your belief. If anyone dares touch you that person would have to pay dearly for it:

   - Isaiah 65: 8
   - Joshua 14: 6,9,10, 1213
   - Ezekiel 9: 12,46 (Ephesians 1:13)
   - Revelation 9: 14 & 11.

2. What is this blessing? How unique is it? It is nothing less than God's throne, i.e. the full deity of God and His heavenly blessings. Because we do not fully trust Him, we always look down on ourselves and give people the chance also to take us for granted. But if you were to have spiritual eyes you would see these blessings. John the Baptist saw the greatness of Jesus when he came to him by the river Jordan. From today, look forward to achieving your greatness:

   - Jeremiah 10: 16
   - Jeremiah 17: 12
   - John 1: 26

3. How to claim these blessings and all others meant for us? By fully trusting in His grace and power for you and also with serious determination.

    - Jeremiah 12: 8
    - Micah 5: 8
    - Ephesians 1: 1821
    - Judges 11: 12 & 24

[B] PRAYER CLAIMS FOR THE blessings

1. We thank God for making us the grace to qualify as His chosen people to share in His blessings.

    - Colossians 1: 12

2. With the power bestowed on us and in Jesus Name we break off every negative yoke against us, our families and against any blessings of ours.

    - Psalm 125: 3
    - Isaiah 52: 1& 2

3. We also break off and deliver ourselves from any link with our family curses.

    - 2 Chronicles 10 16

4. In Jesus Name we now claim every blessing that belong to us in the past, present and future in the same way Caleb claimed his blessings from Joshua.

    - Joshua 14: 6, 910, 1213.
    - Proverbs 6: 30 & 31

5. We invoke God's curse against anyone who opposes our blessings.

    - Jeremiah 12: 14

6. Again thank God for choosing you to display His grace and blessings.

    - Luke 1: 4655

From The Tomb of Arimethea to The Mountain of Galilee

(Matthew 27:5760 & 28:1620)

- WHAT IS THE Tomb OF ARIMETHEA AND WHAT DOES IT DO/AFFECT YOUR LIFE? (MATTHEW 27: 5760;/ 28: 1620)

    It is that situation, time, and place in your life when you lose your blessings and that can make you become 'useless' in life.
    - All visions, purposes, expectations and entire life itself is condemned and buried as expressed by the two disciples on the way to Emmaus (Luke 24: 21)
    - It buries and makes it difficult for what you stand for to manifest (Matthew 27:66).
    - It drives away all that should have been your blessings. Example, all friends leave you since you are no more useful. The disciples of Jesus who even had had courage to stand and witnessed his death on the

cross, after his burial, went home because Jesus was now dead and no more useful as a physical person (Luke 23: 35 & 36)

- It makes sure that you never achieve your blessings. In the tomb of Arimethea, your enemies make every effort every second, minute, hour, day, etc. that you never come out of your troubles (Matthew 27: 6266)

- WHAT LEADS YOU TO THE TOMB?

- You can end up in the tomb by the operations of divine power. This happens because it has been ordained by God, as in the case of Jesus (Psalm 89:48).

- Your own acts/deeds can cause God to send you to the tomb as a punishment ((Ezekiel18:20) (Acts 5: 110)

- Again, your acts/deeds can cause God to send you to the tomb not as a punishment but as a means of saving your soul from hell when as a righteous man you begin to sin (Isaiah 57:1). Or God can take you away to the tomb to save you from physical calamities and pain. Paul at one time wanted God to take him away because of the pain from a disease he was suffering from (2 Cor. 12: 7&8)

- And more foolishly you can send yourself to the tomb through stupid and immoral lifestyle: fornication, drugs, unhealthy eating habits, alcohol, robbery, etc.

- Then the wickedness of this world can send you to the tomb. This can happen by spiritual means: witchcraft, satanic orchestrations, etc. In attempt to kill David the Philistines carried their gods of the battle field to work against and finish him off (2 Samuel 5: 1718, 2021) Or by wrong practices in the society: murder, injustices, wrong accusations, armed robbery, etc. (Matthew 27:1760)

- What IS YOUR MOUNT OF GALILEE AND WHAT HAPPENS THERE? (MATTHEW 28: 1620)
  It is your time and place of ordained blessings.

  - Your life becomes transformed by divine grace and power where rottenness becomes blessings. On the mountain of Galilee, it is the Holy Spirit that deals with your life turning every bit of your life into abundant grace. From the valley/tomb of death, God assumes the operating rod and turns your buried life into resurrecting waters. (Psalm 23: 4), (Jeremiah 31: 40) (Psalm 84: 6&7)

  - Your divinity and hidden nature as God's child become now clear to all in your life. God Himself begins to reveal who you are and advertise you to those around you. You become a point of attention and acceptance instead of despise (Matthew 9: 2836)

  - You are worshipped and celebrated. All that you lost come back to you and are placed at your interest (Matthew 28: 16 & 17).

  - You are now become a vessel of blessing to others. You have so much blessing that you begin to give some out to others (Luke 24: 51)

  - You receive blessings to the extent that you never lack joy. Nothing will take your joy away. Sickness, failure, calamity, poverty, rejection, lack? Never! (Luke 24: 51)

  - You always operate in the power of God which places all other powers, situations, challenges, dominion, etc. under your feet to the extent that we can now judge the twelve tribes of Israel even here on earth (Matthew 28: 1820) (Ephesians 1: 1921), (Daniel 7:27) & (Luke 22: 28)

- **HOW TO GET TO AND REMAIN ON THE MOUNTAIN OF GALILEE?**
  - Believe in every word of God in every sense of the Word, i.e. if exultation, embrace it and if warning, fear it. God is both the Merciful and the Punisher of those who defy Him. Jesus said everything that has been written concerning us will definitely come to pass (Luke 24:44).
  - Make it a habit to study, understand and remember always the Word of God. That would place you in a position to know what God is saying concerning what relates to your life and live by it. (Luke 24: 47)
  - Most importantly live and do/act as directed by God's Word, i.e. act on the Word (Matthew 28: 10 & 16)
  - Worship God always in any way you can: songs, sacrifices, meditation, godly lively, tithing, etc. (Matthew 28: 17)

www.ingramcontent.com/pod-product-compliance
Lightning Source LLC
Chambersburg PA
CBHW030521080526
44586CB00011B/274